Glide Projection

Lateral Architectural Drawing

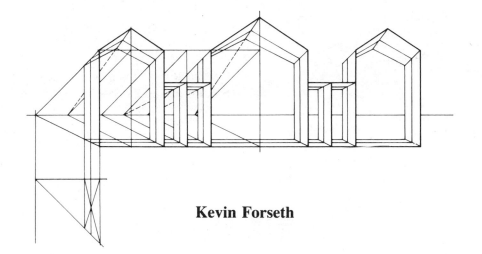

Kevin Forseth

 Van Nostrand Reinhold Company

Library of Congress Catalog Card Number 84-7559

ISBN 0-442-22674-8 (cloth)
ISBN 0-442-22672-1 (paper)

Printed in the United States of America

Designed by Kevin Forseth

Published by Van Nostrand Reinhold Company Inc.
135 West 50th Street
New York, New York 10020

Van Nostrand Reinhold Company Limited
Molly Millars Lane
Wokingham, Berkshire RG11 2PY, England

Van Nostrand Reinhold
480 La Trobe Street
Melbourne, Victoria 3000, Australia

Macmillan of Canada
Division of Gage Publishing Limited
164 Commander Boulevard
Agincourt, Ontario M1S 3C7, Canada

16 15 14 13 12 11 10 9 8 7 6 5 4 3 2 1

Library of Congress Cataloging in Publication Data

Forseth, Kevin.
  Glide projection.

  Includes index.
  1. Perspective. 2. Measured drawing. I. Title.
NA2710.F6 1984 720'.28'4   84-7559
ISBN 0-442-22674-8
ISBN 0-442-22672-1 (pbk.)

Acknowledgments

This book was supported by a grant from the Graham Foundation for Advanced Studies in the Fine Arts.

I would like to thank the following people for their help in preparing this book: Eric Palson, who inspired the idea and provided several of the written passages for the first chapter; Michael Garber, who drafted the complex precision drawings; Robert Ruggles and Linda Estkowski, who illustrated the scenographic tone drawings; and Wendy Lochner, who provided insightful criticism during the editing of the manuscript.

I am also grateful to the faculty and students at the University of Wisconsin–Milwaukee School of Architecture and Urban Planning for providing the setting for this sort of idea to evolve.

This book is dedicated to my wife, Katie, who patiently supported me through the ordeal of putting everything together.

Contents

Preface

This book explains a new and useful system of measured pictorial drawing called glide projection. Named after the distinctive way in which they focus images, glide drawings are intended to complement the conventional range of pictorial drawing constructions. For centuries, the two most common graphic methods, perspectives and paralines, have effectively depicted the views of objects and surfaces only as they appear in the context of space. The purpose of glide drawings is to depict the opposite of this spatial view — in other words, to show built-up forms within the context of broad and shallow surfaces.

All material for this book is presented in nonmathematical terms, requiring only an acquaintance with the methods and procedures of linear perspective in order to be applied and understood. Due to the ease with which glides can be learned, and due to the fact that glides effectively structure the views of many different situations — from long and narrow street facades to aerial views of gardens to shallow sections and floor plans, to certain trompe l'oeil effects — glide drawings should appeal to designers in many fields, from architecture to interior design, landscape architecture, art, and urban design.

Much of the reason for linear perspective's enduring success can be attributed to the fact that for centuries its principles have been transmitted from person to person or from book to person on both procedural and theoretical levels. Procedural linear-perspective techniques, handed down to us in the form of treatises on rules and conventions since the days of Alberti, provide us with painless means for expedient application but at the expense of any real intellectual appreciation of perspective principles. On the other hand, theoretical linear perspective, in taking us beyond requisite skill levels to the foundations of perspective projection, is simply beyond the grasp of the casual user. Regarded positively, the delightful consequence of these stratified learning approaches is that linear perspective has always offered something for everybody to understand.

In keeping with the flavor of this perspective model, the main chapters of this book are devoted to glide-drawing methods and glide-projection theory. For readers who are intent upon quickly applying glide principles, I recommend reading the glide-drawing chapter first. The glide-application chapter supplements this approach. For readers in search of enlightenment, I recommend reading the first two chapters, followed by the chapter on glide projection.

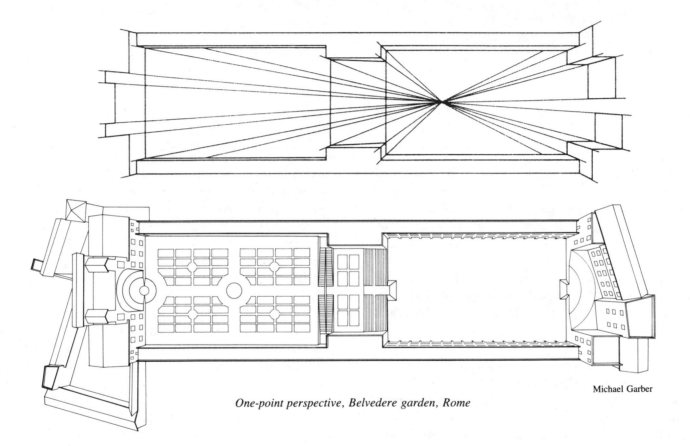

One-point perspective, Belvedere garden, Rome

Michael Garber

Introduction

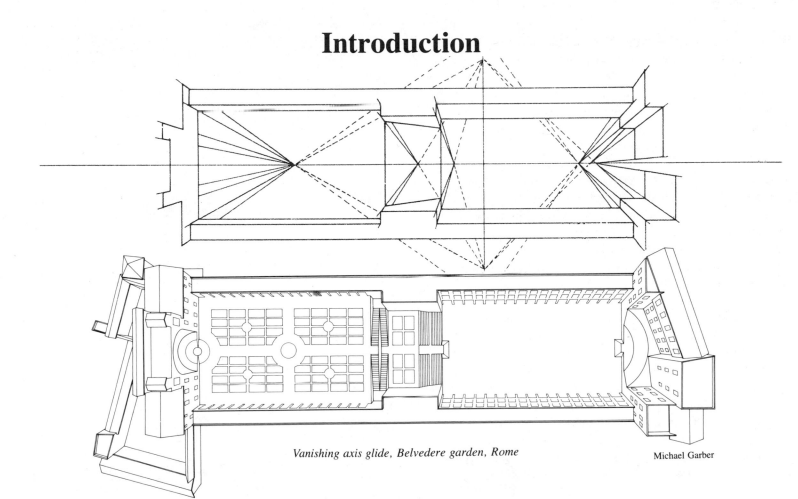

Vanishing axis glide, Belvedere garden, Rome

Michael Garber

The problem involved constructing an aerial one-point perspective view looking down upon the site plan of an Italian formal garden. Michael, the student who was working with me at the time, was searching for the clearest way to express the garden's three-dimensional form. However, after several futile attempts, it became apparent that no matter how he chose to structure its image, significant graphic tradeoffs and unwarranted compromises were involved; conventional drawing methods were not adequate graphic tools for describing the garden's overall form.

Because of the long and narrow shape of the garden, one-point perspective constructions were ineffective. Garden endwalls and sidewalls competed for correct visual expression, with the result that no perspective setup satisfactorily revealed the essential surface details of the garden walls without noticeable visual distortion.

Four different pictorial views of the same long and narrow rectangular courtyard are shown at right. Two of these constructions illustrate the one-point perspective dilemma. Note that in both of the perspective constructions, the center vanishing point determines the line or edge along which adjacent perimeter wall planes must meet. Because the courtyard is rectangular and not square, the constructed widths of end- and sidewalls cannot be made equal. In fact, the narrower the rectangular courtyard, the greater the difference in the projected widths of the perimeter walls. Thus, if the long sidewalls are made wide enough in the perspective view to see details such as windows and arches upon their surfaces, then the endwalls will appear very deep and the overall aerial view will not suggest a shallow space. On the other hand, if a shallow width for the endwalls is first constructed, then virtually no surface detail will be seen on the resulting narrow sidewalls.

Paraline constructions, both normal and split variations, were also ineffective. Normal paralines revealed only two of the garden's internal wall surfaces within a single view, making it necessary to construct two views in order to see the detail on all four internal walls. Split paralines solved this problem but created another. In effect, a split paraline is two separate paralines that mirror each other across a central axis. All internal walls can be seen at once, but if the floor level changes within a split paraline, there is a wedge of space along the central axis that is undefined, resulting in a sectional view through the changing floor levels.

The garden construction problem was finally solved with a vanishing axis construction. This construction brought the perspective dilemma into balance by revealing all four of the garden's internal walls in controlled proportion to one another. It also eliminated the split-paraline problem by making the space continuous across the center axis. The perspective central vanishing point had dissolved into a vanishing axis.

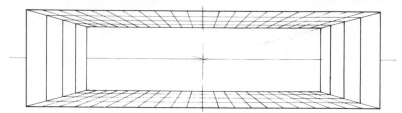

One-point perspective: endwalls distorted

One-point perspective: sidewalls too shallow

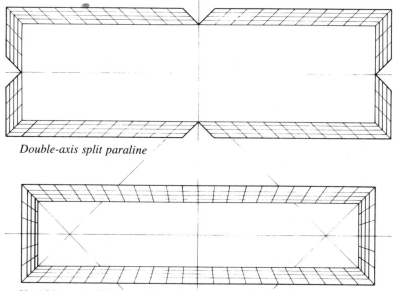

Double-axis split paraline

Vanishing axis glide: equal emphasis on all four walls

Soon after developing the geometry of the vanishing axis construction, other related drawing variations evolved. Some contained vanishing planes instead of vanishing axes; others combined vanishing planes and axes within the same pictorial image. All were governed by the principles of a more general projective order, a system conceptually different than perspective or paraline. Further, the geometry underlying these variations suggested an altogether different way of viewing their illusions. Unlike perspective constructions, which are meant to be optically viewed from the static vantage of a single spectator position, vanishing axis and vanishing plane images are structured to be laterally scanned from the dynamic vantage of a continuous viewing plane.

This unique viewing condition inspired the name for the family of all vanishing axis and plane variations. Thus, the term "glide" describes how the eye of a spectator physically glides parallel to the surface of such constructions in order to accurately read their projected images.

Double-slit Projection

From the beginning, it seemed important to keep the rules and procedures for generating pictorial constructions simple, for if they became complex, no reasonable person would care to use the system. The problem with difficult procedures is brought out in the case of double-slit projections.

There is a way in which to focus images that is neither glide, perspective, nor paraline. Developed while working on glide theory, it was named double-slit projection for the way that it focused the

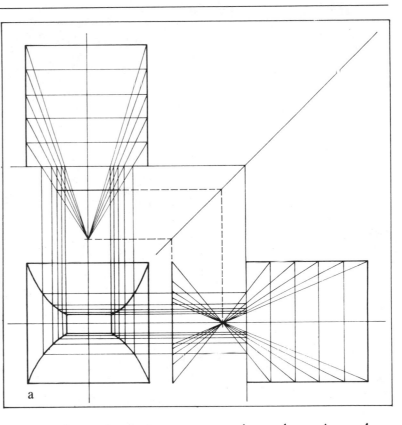

a

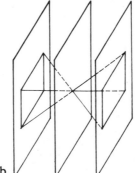

b

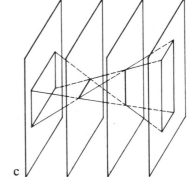

c

a. *Double-slit image projected from top and side views of a cube*
b. *The geometry of point projection requires one focal plane*
c. *Double-slit projection requires two planes*

9

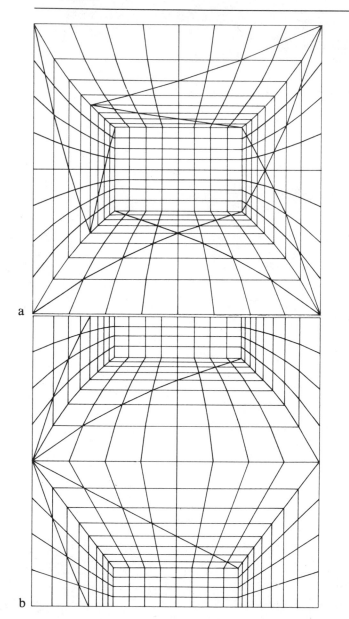

a. *Double-slit construction*
b. *Double-slit image compared with vanishing-axis construction*

image of an object onto the surface of a picture plane by means of two slits oriented perpendicular to one another. Its image resembles a normal perspective view that has been stretched along one axis.

In terms of its structural and visual properties, double-slit projection is similar to vanishing-axis glide projection, yet it is different in one important respect. Many of the lines within a double-slit construction appear to curve, making its construction impractical.

Glide Field Assumption

Glides are based on a different field assumption than paralines and perspectives. Early drafts of this book often referred to glides as compressed spatial constructions. Gradually, however, it became apparent that the spatial field, a real situation, had nothing to do with the idea of projective system, an uninterpreted logical structure. Thus, the orderly way in which points are transferred to the surface of the picture plane, which is another way of describing a projective system, is not related to our interpretation of the nature of the setting in which the view takes place. Projection systems may be used interchangeably for the purpose of depicting spatial or surface fields, but the system of perspective projection is structured to depict spatial situations with greater clarity than glide projection, and glides are structured to show surface conditions with greater clarity than perspectives. Space and surface are different open-ended field assumptions. Glide and perspective are different internally consistent projection systems. The nature of this glide visual field and its relation to the perspective field are described in more detail in the following chapter.

10

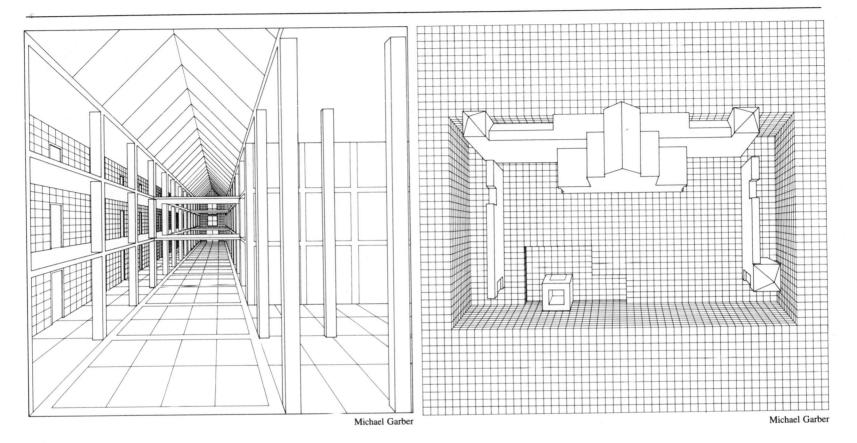

Michael Garber

Michael Garber

One-point perspective view into deep spatial corridor

Vanishing-axis glide view of broad and shallow surface

Glide As An Alternative To Perspective

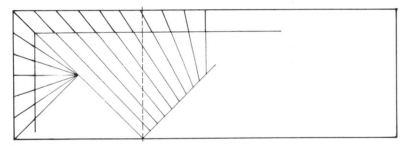

G. Viola-Zanini's traveling-vanishing-point construction

Vanishing-axis Constructions

In 1629, G. Viola-Zanini, an Italian architect and painter, devoted several pages of his treatise on linear perspective to an account of a construction method based on the idea of a traveling vanishing point. The method, which was intended to correct for visual distor-

tion within long and narrow ceiling perspectives, actually worked, and was used by many of the painters of his era. In outward appearance, Zanini's vanishing-axis construction resembled a normal one-point perspective, conveying the illusion of lines vanishing towards the middle of the composition. In fact, few of its receding parallels ever did meet at the center point because they vanished along an axis instead.

Even though the traveling-vanishing-point construction was useful, Zanini's method never gained public acceptance. There were several good reasons for this. For one thing, his vanishing-axis structure contradicted one of the basic laws of linear perspective, which stated that all related parallels must vanish to a point. Few people during the 17th century were of a mind to deal with the seemingly absurd consequences of this contradiction. For another, Zanini's method described outward pictorial effects only. His method was not supported with a general theory, nor did its geometry have a basis in optical phenomena.

With no theory or demonstration to support its application, the vanishing-axis construction was easily discredited by the leading perspective theorists of the Renaissance. Afraid that its acceptance would lead to perspective liberties, Andrea Pozzo, a renowned scenographic painter, appended a portion of his treatise on perspective, written in 1693, to assert his disdain for such constructions. By the end of the 17th century, Zanini's traveling-vanishing-point construction had faded into obscurity.

Zanini's method was not without precedent. Vanishing-axis and vanishing-plane constructions were relevant pictorial effects through much of history. They were conventional in the Middle Ages and can be found in ancient mural constructions as well.

The Roman architect Vitruvius defined a suitable picture as the realistic image of something that could or did exist in the physical world. Following his lead, the painters of the architectural wall murals of ancient Pompeii made use of many different pictorial vanishing patterns. Three of these patterns consisted of geometries in which related depth parallels appeared to vanish to a point or along a line, or remain parallel.

The perspective effect achieved by leading the eye to a single vanishing point was used to structure one of the scenographic wall paintings in the House of the Labyrinth. In this painting, the surface of the wall appears to dissolve into the distant prospect of illusionistic space beyond, and receding lines appear to nearly but not exactly converge towards a common point.

Paraline construction, Pentheus Room, House of the Vettii, Pompeii

Robert Ruggles

Robert Ruggles

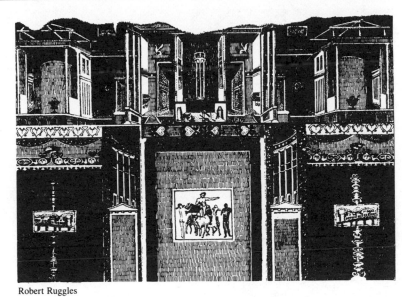

Robert Ruggles

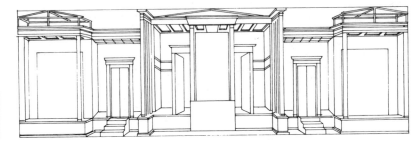

One-point construction, the House of the Labyrinth, Pompeii

Vanishing-axis construction, House of Marcus Lucretius Fronto, Pompeii

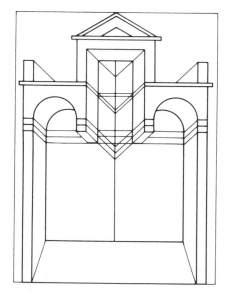

A wall panel in the House of the Vettii, Pentheus Room, depicts the paraline view of a pavilion silhouetted against the sky. Although the viewing angle would be interpreted differently today, the fact that depth parallels remain parallel attests to the distinctive paraline flavor of this illusion.

The wall detail from the House of Marcus Lucretius Fronto is patterned after yet another suitable pictorial effect, the vanishing-axis construction. John White, in his book *The Birth and Rebirth of Pictorial Space,* written in 1957, describes the behavior of its receding lines: ". . . as early as the Second-style decoration of the summer triclinium at Boscoreale, those lines which do not actually converge towards a single point tend to recede in pairs towards a vanishing axis" (p. 265).

The vanishing-axis pictorial effect was natural for the shape of its enclosing frame, which was a rather long and narrow wall. Parallels in depth met along an axis, though in no orderly way.

The same pictorial effects — vanishing point, line, and parallel — along with several other variations, were used interchangeably during late Antique, Byzantine and Medieval ages. Typical of the art of the ages is the Scene from the St. Cecilia Altarpiece, with lines that appear to vanish along an axis.

In recent times, vanishing-axis constructions have been used only sparingly. They are not mentioned in textbooks on pictorial graphic constructions, and on the rare occasions when their pictorial effects are seen in illustrations, such as those from *The House Book* by

Scene from the St. Cecilia Altarpiece

16

Terence Conran, it is as if they were used as a last resort or in the spirit of rebellion, not with a strong sense of conviction. The fact that Conran's illustrations were not labeled attests to the vagueness of the convention; yet, even when these constructions are labeled, the results can be ambiguous. A form of vanishing-axis site plan, found in a book written by Paolo Portoghesi in 1982, is labeled axonometric, although it clearly is not. Rudolfo Machado's bedroom (*Country House,* 1977) is another example of a vanishing-axis construction of sorts, labeled sectional perspective.

Zanini's method was intended to correct for a particular perspective distortion. Implicit in his approach was the attitude that vanishing-axis constructions were a mere remedy for optical problems on the fringes of perspective respectability, to be dealt with as particular problems arose, an attitude that has carried over to the present day. Arcane artistic implications aside, it would seem that for centuries vanishing-axis drawings have been treated as mere graphic first aid for minor perspective blemishes.

Vanishing-axis constructions resemble what we are here calling glide drawings. More than just a remedial technique for perspective phenomena, the system of glide drawings is a complete and coherent projective order, intended to unify a diverse range of pictorial effects, including traveling vanishing point, vanishing plane, herringbone, eggcrate, pigeonhole, and reverse perspective. Each of these glide variations, accepted as convention during various periods in ancient and medieval history, was abandoned without explanation during the Renaissance in favor of perspective and paraline structures.

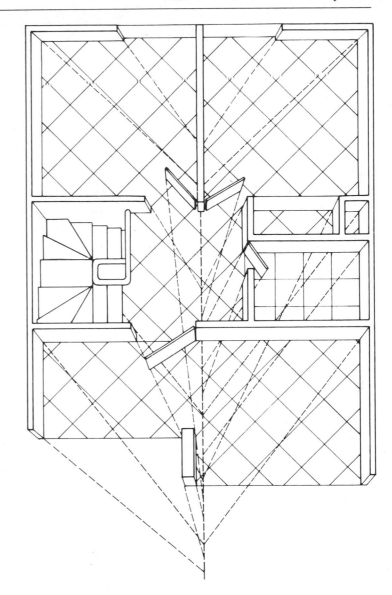

After Terence Conran, scaled herringbone-glide construction

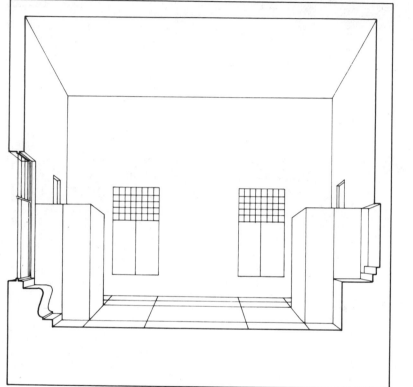

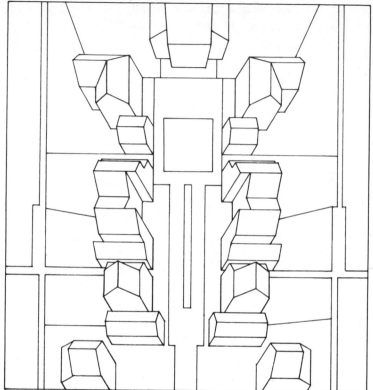

After Rudolfo Machado, sectional perspective, bedroom, Country House, 1977

After Francis Ceria and Alain Coupel, axonometric plan (scaled herringbone), Plan de L'Eglise, New Town of St-Quentin-en-Yvelines

The Origins of Linear Perspective

For five hundred years, linear perspective has been the dominant, some would say only pictorial projective form. During that time glides have not evolved much beyond the conventions of their Roman and medieval precedents. How did this happen? With the rediscovery of perspective during the Renaissance, various philosophical obstacles prevented glides from ever again being taken seriously as a legitimate mode of pictorial representation.

In light of the importance of events surrounding the rediscovery of perspective, especially as these events may have conspired to shape our collective sense of pictorial appropriateness even today, it is worth briefly considering some of the more general and persistent influences that might have affected the development of glide drawings during the Renaissance.

The Choice of Perspective

Linear perspective was rediscovered around 1425 by the great Florentine architect, Philipo Brunelleschi. If we pause to reflect upon the significance of the achievement, it is obvious that Brunelleschi, as the first to propose a system of pictorial projection, was not encumbered by the influence of his own discovery. In other words, he was free at the time to develop all the pictorial alternatives from the past, not just perspective. Why, then, we might reasonably wonder, did he choose to develop only perspective? Why weren't other projective forms, including glides, demonstrated at the same time? In my opinion, a reasonable explanation for Brunelleschi's actions would have to focus upon the pervasive philosophical attitudes that in-spired artists of the Renaissance to develop perspective in the first place.

For instance, it is entirely possible that Brunelleschi's decision to develop only perspective was influenced by aspects of his humanist background. In promoting the welfare of a certain group of upwardly mobile people, humanism advocated the then-bold idea that the quality of life for each individual here in this world was of far greater significance than previous social philosophies were willing to consider.

The humanist dictum, ''Man is the measure of all things,'' not only captured the flavor of the Renaissance, it also captured the essence of the then-new pictorial drawing convention, perspective. The relation between humanist doctrine and perspective illusion was first expressed in Alberti's treatise, *Della Pittura*, written in 1436. In his treatise, the oldest text to describe a method of perspective construction, Alberti stressed that the appearances of all things were relative and that the human figure alone provided the measure of things seen or depicted.

Single-vantage linear perspective was well adapted to the presentation of surrounding space on a scale in which the individual was significant, potentially dominant. It was the singular view as seen from the ground. It was the view of the architect and of his patron.

In contrast, glides are a convention of continuity, descriptive of the group and not the individual; they sacrifice strong evocation of being at a particular place for a clear mapping of a collection of impressions of places. Glide projection, by virtue of multiple vantage points, describes subjects on a scale that exceeds a single experience. Effects produced in various areas can be judged simultaneously. It is a decentralized convention that can describe entities too large to be considered as a single unit.

There can be little doubt that linear perspective reflected the prevailing humanist attitudes of the Renaissance. Yet, while we may accept the fact that linear perspective conformed with humanist ideals more completely than any other projective order, we may wonder why Renaissance theorists chose to exclude all but one pictorial system from consideration. It may be that perspective was the preferred pictorial system for the majority of uses at that time, but this is not a license for exclusivity.

Rationalism and the Problem of Alternative Structures

Humanism as a materialist philosophy stressed intellectual powers over emotion, the sensual richness of the classical past over medieval spirituality. In choosing reason over intuition, humanists adopted the classical writings of Plato. Brunelleschi, who rediscovered perspective, and Alberti, who first wrote about it, accepted the Platonic interpretation of geometric structure, which considered the objects studied by geometry to be real but not of this world. In conceding that the mind existed outside the body, Plato allowed for a world of transcendent perfect forms that served to explain the underlying structure of the temporal and particular forms of everyday life. Thus, Brunelleschi, Alberti, and other humanists of the Renaissance shared in the belief that perspective represented a universal order, more significant and everlasting than the fleeting particulars of everyday human existence and perception.

Piero Della Francesca, an Italian Renaissance painter, was thinking like a rationalist when he wrote: "Therefore, I say perspective is necessary; because as a true science it distinguishes degrees of size in proportional terms, by showing the foreshortening and enlarging of every size by means of lines. Observing this, many ancient painters acquired eternal fame, like Aristomenes of Thasos, Polycles, Appelles-Andramides, Nitheusm Zeuxis, and many others. Although many without perspective are given praise, this has been done with poor judgement by those who have no knowledge of the possibility of art."

Piero had strong feelings regarding the a priori status of linear perspective. Of course, in advocating this rationalist interpretation of perspective geometry, Francesca implicity excluded the possibility of alternatives. In the end, because he was a rationalist, Francesca could conceive of only one real and necessary pictorial system; and because he was a humanist, that system was perspective.

The rationalist interpretation of perspective geometry was accepted for a very long time, at least partly because linear perspective was slow to shed its associations with the physical world. Surprisingly, during the time of Alberti, perspective was not understood as a purely deductive projective system, because many of its elements and principles were woven in with aspects of the real world. The noninductive nature of perspective geometry was not understood until centuries later after a slow process of abstraction.

The gradual evolution of an independent theory of perspective projection is most intriguing. More than one hundred years after the rediscovery of perspective, Jean Cousin became the first to define accidental vanishing points as points of convergence for related parallels but only for lines converging towards the horizon. Forty years after Cousin's treatise, Giubaldo del Monte became the first to develop a full convergence-point theory, one that defined the vanishing point for every set of related parallels, not just those vanishing towards the horizon line. Yet, even after 1700, the ground plane remained a necessary perspective element. It wasn't until 1715 that Brook Taylor finally freed perspective of its last contextual vestiges, expressing it as an independent system of picture plane and projectors. After that, perspective became increasingly more abstract and general, until in 1813 Jean-Victor Poncelet formulated the basic postulates of projective geometry.

Soon after Poncelet's formulations, the rationalist interpretation of perspective projection was shaken at its foundations with the invention of other projective geometries, among which were Lobachevski and Bolyai's hyperbolic geometry and Reimann's elliptical geometry. To the dismay of perspective rationalists, hyperbolic and elliptical geometries, both of which were internally consistent systems of projection, were based upon different interpretations of the parallel postulate, thus contradicting the universal principles of perspective.

The discovery of alternative non-Euclidean geometries cast serious doubt upon rationalist perspective theory. How could perspective be both factual and necessary when it was possible to conceive of alternatives? A satisfactory solution to the dilemma of alternative projective geometries had to wait until the 19th and early 20th centuries, when mathematicians such as Klein and Hilbert were able to provide a logical basis for multiple geometries. It is on the basis of their theories that we are able to conceive of glides as an alternative to perspectives today.

In order to set the stage for the inclusion of nonperspective glide projection, let us return briefly to the early Renaissance. Humanists such as Alberti and Brunelleschi may have interpreted perspective in terms of the universal ideals of Platonic rationalism, but they were not averse to confirming the truth of their theories with demonstrations. Thus, while they surely admired Plato, they nonetheless rejected the notion that truth could be established purely by argument.

Alberti is said to have amazed the citizens of Florence with his perspective devices. His pictures ''brought about things unheard of and that the spectators found unbelievable, and he showed these things through a tiny opening that was made in a little closed box. He called these things 'demonstrations' and they were of such a kind that both artists and laymen questioned whether they saw painted things or natural things themselves'' (author anonymous, *Vita anonima*, 15th century).

A few years before Alberti's demonstrations, Brunelleschi was the first to experimentally verify the true point-projective nature of linear perspective. This he did with a mirror and panel. The results of his experiment provided compelling observational evidence in support of perspective conventions.

Alberti and Brunelleschi were thus aware of both the system of perspective geometry and its demonstration. However, and this is very important, as Platonic rationalists they placed greater faith in the geometry than they did in the results of their demonstrations.

Remarkably, the problem of accommodating alternative projective structures, which was brought about by the 19th century invention of non-Euclidean geometries, involved shifting the emphasis of significance from dubious universal geometric structures to the demonstrated properties of the systems. Those who placed greater significance on the truth of their demonstrations than on the truth of the geometric systems that conformed with the results of their experiments were called empiricists.

The Empirical Interpretation of Perspective Projection

Empirical knowledge, as defined by philosophers such as Bacon and Hume, consists of two kinds of knowledge, what we know by direct observation of the real world through our eyes and other senses and what we know by generalization or hypothesis. Such knowledge may be in scientific form or as rough and unsystematic as conclusions drawn from everyday experience, but what matters is that only knowledge of the first kind is unquestionably true.

Regarding knowledge of the second kind — linear perspective, for example — can be divided into two empirical categories, its uninterpreted and its interpreted systems. As an uninterpreted system, linear perspective is nothing more than an empty geometric game, conceived by the human mind, that asserts nothing of significance about the real world of experience. Abstract terms such as "picture plane," "projector ray," and "image point" belong to the uninterpreted system of perspective projection.

Brunelleschi's experiment with mirror and panel

a. Mirror
b. Panel

The empiricist is free to conceive of projective geometries, as an uninterpreted system, without any reference to actual experience. Contradictions between systems do not present any problems because the systems themselves are merely nominal games. Such purely deductive, internally consistent geometric structures can be put together with symbols, formation rules, definitions, and axioms and yet have no external reference until they are applied to some real situation.

Uninterpreted systems of the sort mentioned above take on significance when they are interpreted in terms of the real and physical world. As soon as meanings are assigned to their symbols, these projective systems are transformed from mere games of logic into testable hypotheses about aspects of reality. Thus, when a pure projective system such as perspective is interpreted in terms of the physical world, its formal structure hypothetically models the behavior of phenomena such as light optics, and its system becomes factual within testable errors of measurement.

Ultimately, what was confusing about perspective as it was studied by the humanists, and what made it seem so compellingly certain and informative to generations of perspective theorists after the Renaissance, was that it simultaneously combined pure and applied geometries. Empiricists, in separating pure from applied geometries and in emphasizing the significance of their applied aspects, were able to conceive of alternative projective systems without fear of contradicting established principles.

System, Interpretation, and Demonstration

From an empiricist's point of view, the geometry for a projection system such as perspective or glide must be shown to be internally consistent. But even if free of internal contradiction, the projective system will remain a meaningless game of rules if not interpreted in terms of the real world. If interpreted, its principles can be demonstrated to be true. This applies to every projective system, including glides and perspectives. Towards that end, we shall need to develop two interpretive systems, one for perspective that is compatible with glide, and one for glide that can be demonstrated to be true.

Let's begin with a brief review of the interpreted system of perspective projection. Perspective was adopted with a passion during the Renaissance not only because its principles could be demonstrated to be true but because its geometry was modeled after the focusing structure of the human eye. For Brunelleschi, it would have seemed impossible to conceive of a system of visual projection that did not in some way relate to the optics of the seeing eye, and since the system of perspective projection was patterned after the very way that every individual eye focused images, what other system could there be? Even if there were alternative systems, how could they possibly be truer than perspective? For seemingly obvious optical reasons, perspective was therefore favored as the only conceivable pictorial projective alternative.

The apparent truth of this optical argument ignores subtle but important interpretations of perspective structure. Then, as now, certain aspects were taken for granted, aspects so obvious as to be overlooked. One such overlooked interpretation of perspective structure can be explained in terms of a condition of Brunelleschi's original perspective experiment. In this experiment, the perspective illusion was meant to be viewed from a single point in space, as if through a peephole. Brunelleschi seems to have implicitly understood that the

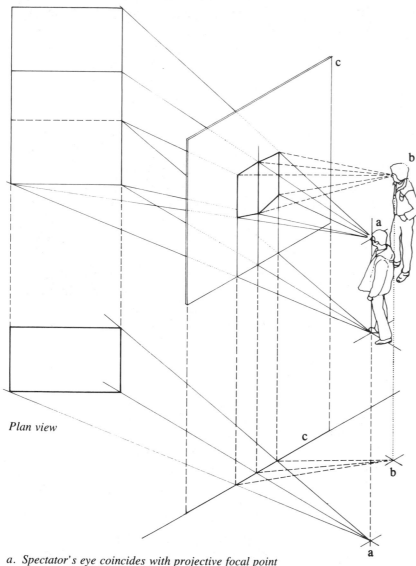

Plan view

a. Spectator's eye coincides with projective focal point
b. Spectator's eye does not coincide with focal point
c. Picture plane

perspective illusion would faithfully represent the depicted scene only if the spectator viewing the illusion was positioned so that his or her eye coincided with the focal center of the original projection. From all other viewing stations the illusion would not be optically accurate and some degree of visual distortion would occur. Soon thereafter, perspectives were constructed without regard for this condition. Spectators began viewing completed perspective illusions from general areas in front of paintings rather than always through pinholes.

Because very few perspective projections are viewed from their original focal centers, justification for interpreting the truth of linear perspective on the basis of its relation to the focal structure of the human eye is somewhat tenuous.

On the basis of the subtle distinction between actual and spectator viewing circumstances, we may interpret two kinds of perspective illusions: distorted and undistorted. Either the spectator's eye coincides with the original projective focal point, in which case the entire illusion appears undistorted, or the spectator's eye is located somewhere else in front of the illusion, in which case the entire view appears distorted to some degree.

Glides mediate these perspective extremes. In reducing distortion within illusions meant to be scanned rather than focused, the glide view can be interpreted as consisting of many local optically correct views, with no central optically true vantage position. Thus, if perspective is useful for bringing entire scenes together as wholes, glides can be thought of as useful for bringing fragments of entire scenes together in sequences.

The interpretive differences between perspectives and glides can be stated in more precise terms, but before we define these terms, let us describe a typical perspective projection.

The Perspective Demonstration

The idea that a perspective drawing can be interpreted as the projected image of figures in space has been understood for over five hundred years. Among early treatises on perspective, the 16th-century woodcuts and engravings of Albrecht Dürer are exceptional for the clarity with which they demonstrate the idea of projection. His prints, those in which the use of some mechanical apparatus is illustrated, are useful even today in gaining insight into the essential structure and setting for perspective projection. In a typical scene, staged to resemble a demonstration, an artist stands before a hinged canvas or gridded plane with a vase or musical instrument resting on a table behind the picture frame. The perspective drawing made by the artist is the projection of the vase or lute onto the plane of the canvas, with the center of projection at the eye of the artist.

Although it is not commonly thought to matter, there is an important distinction to be made between actual and spectator projections. One type of projection is used in the process of generating illusions, the other in viewing their completed images. An actual projection, which generates pictorial images, brings the illusion on the picture plane into correspondence with figures and surfaces in space by means of orderly arrangements of projectors. The arrangement of actual projectors varies from one drawing type to another so that in the special case of an actual perspective projection, the projectors are arranged to meet at a central point; with paraline and glide projections, the arrangement of projectors is different. Regardless of individual structure, actual projections can be thought of as uninterpreted systems whose only purpose is to bring order to the relation between image and setting.

Albrecht Dürer: A man drawing a vase, *1538*

Albrecht Dürer: Draughtsman Making a Perspective Drawing of a Woman, *1525*

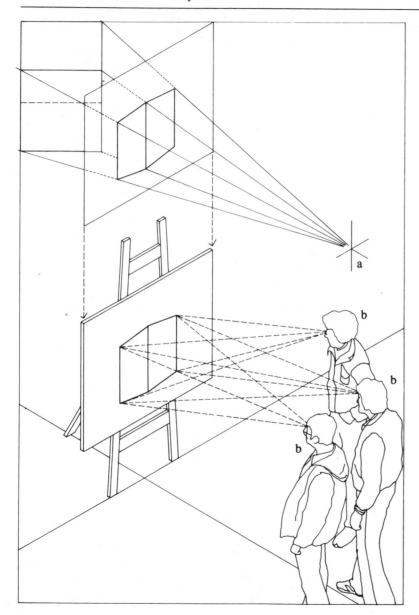

a. *Actual projection*
b. *Spectator projection*

Spectator projection is entirely different than actual projection. Modeled after the workings of the human eye, every spectator projection is point-projective. No other order is conceivable. Spectator projectors extend only from the eye of the viewer to the surface of the picture plane, never beyond. This, of course, is brought about because the physical surface of a viewed pictorial illusion is always opaque.

Optical and Pictorial Resemblance Views

An optical view, which in the case of perspective is the only true view, is seen only by the spectator whose eye coincides exactly with the center projective point of the actual perspective projection. When viewed from this special point, the plane of the perspective illusion seems to dissolve into the depicted space beyond its surface, as if observed in reality. Optical views replicate the precise disposition of lines and planes in space, becoming windows onto the world beyond the surface of their illusions. There is only one position from which to view an optically correct perspective image. In the Dürer print, an optically correct perspective view of the reclining model is seen by the artist with his eye at the tip of the obelisk.

A pictorial view is that seen by a spectator whose eye does not coincide exactly with the original location of the perspective projective point. The viewed perspective illusion will usually be pictorial. In fact, it is the rare case in which an illusion is viewed only from its true projective focal point. Generally, perspectives are viewed from somewhere in front of and in line with the center of the composition, from pictorial viewing stations, from points that do not precisely coincide with the true projective center.

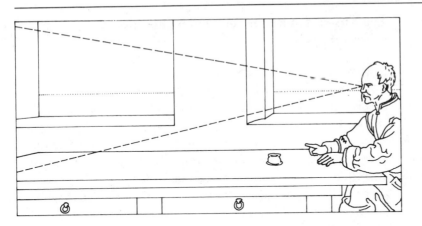

Spectator projection

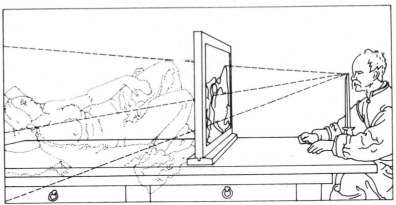

Optical view

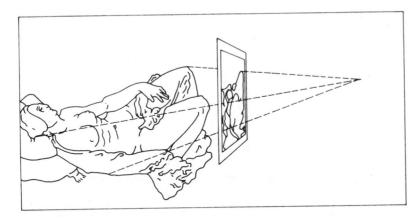

Actual Projection

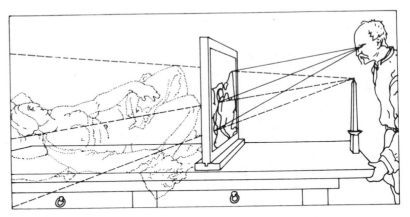

Pictorial resemblance view

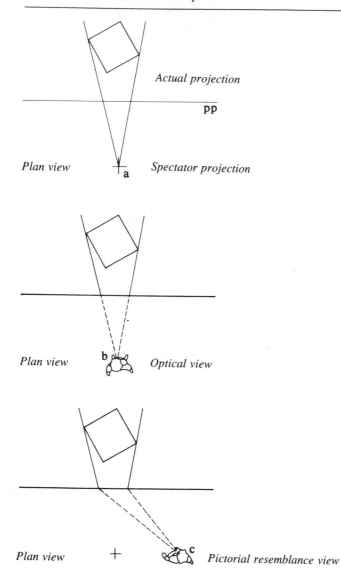

Actual projection

pp

Plan view   a   *Spectator projection*

Plan view   b   *Optical view*

Plan view   +   c   *Pictorial resemblance view*

The Abstracted System of Actual and Spectator Projectors

If the three-dimensional arrangement of projectors and picture plane is viewed in plan only, with the picture plane seen in edge view, then the distinction between actual and spectator rays can be seen quite clearly. Projection lines that occur behind the picture plane are called actual projector rays. Actual projection rays connect points in space to the surface of the picture plane. The projectors in front of the picture plane are spectator rays. Each of these rays connects points on the picture plane with the eye of the person viewing the pictorial illusion. By making the distinction between actual and spectator projector rays in this way, the important difference between projectors that are used to generate pictorial images and projectors that are used to view them after they are completed is reduced to a simple arrangement of lines behind and in front of the picture plane.

Referring to the plan diagram, with actual rays located behind and spectator rays located in front of the picture plane, the distinction between optical and pictorial resemblance views can now be described in terms of whether the paths of continuous projector rays appear to bend or remain straight as they cross the surface of the picture plane. An optical view, where the spectator's eye coincides with the actual projective focus of the illusion, preserves the straight path of every single projector ray through the picture plane. Each continuous projector ray, which consists of spectator and actual components, does not appear to bend at the surface of the picture plane. In such viewing situations, the shape and location of the picture plane theoretically do not matter because no bending of rays occurs at its surface to suggest its presence. The location of the picture plane is unimportant when the spectator's eye is coincident with the actual center projection point.

28

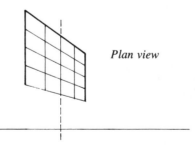

Plan view

Ames room demonstration

In pictorial views, the spectator and center projective points are separated from one another. By implication, projection lines appear to bend at the surface of the picture plane. The actual projection lines behind the picture plane focus on the actual projection point. But since the illusion is viewed by a spectator whose vantage position does not coincide with the actual projective center, actual projective lines appear to bend at the surface of the picture plane in order to focus on the displaced spectator's projection point. The position of the plane of the perspective illusion matters in such cases, for bending of projectors occurs at its interface. In such cases, the plane of the perspective illusion assumes a positive presence. Its surface begins to matter. Obviously, this bending varies depending upon the position of the spectator. We have learned to "read" perspective illusions where bending of projectors occurs, which is theoretically the case with all pictorial viewing situations.

Distortion and Deception

Distortion and deception are the enemies of illusionistic accuracy. Deception occurs through manipulation of elements within the visual field; distortion occurs whenever the view is pictorial rather than actual.

Although illusionistic deception does not enter directly into an understanding of glide phenomena, it is worth mentioning. Deception occurs when illusions seem other than what they are. An example of such a deceptive illusion would be the Ames room, where the viewer is led to believe that he is seeing an illusion of a normal room in perspective through a peephole. In reality, the shape of the room is quite different. Another example would be the seemingly paraline illusion of a cube that turns out to be the projection of disjointed planes in space. In both cases, it is the arrangement of elements in the field that makes the illusion work. Many artists have played with the idea of illusionistic deception, among them William Hogarth.

An example of illusionistic deception through manipulation of elements in the visual field

Paraline projection of disjointed planes in space

Distortion is quite different. In abstract terms, distortion occurs as the result of spectator viewing positions that do not coincide with the original focus of projection. Two characteristics should be emphasized: it occurs in all nonoptical pictorial viewing situations, no matter what the projective structure, no matter what the shape of the picture plane; and it occurs in degrees, with no clear boundary defining greater or lesser distortion.

Anamorphic drawings are a good example of distorted perspective illusions. In order to "see" the undistorted view of an anamorphic drawing, the spectator must view from a very unnatural position off to the side of the picture, where the actual position of the drawing's central projective point is intentionally located in order to fool the spectator.

The degree of distortion is directly related to the extent of bending that occurs between spectator and actual projectors. The greater the bend, the greater the distortion. In the case of optical perspective, there is no bend in projectors as they cross the surface of the picture plane and therefore no distortion. On the other hand, the well-known practice of limiting the perspective visual field to 20° or 30°, based on the tacit assumption that the perspective illusion is pictorial rather than optical, is intended to remedy the problem of distortion at the edge of the perspective view, where the bending of spectator and actual projectors is greatest.

Most perspectives are viewed pictorially. All pictorial views are distorted to a greater or lesser extent. Distortion generally occurs toward the perimeter of a perspective construction, away from its center. Glide projections are intended to reduce the degree of distortion within certain pictorial perspective views.

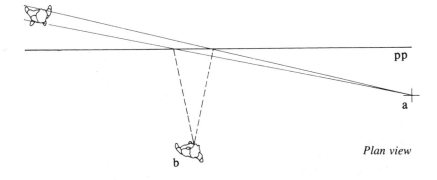

Anamorphic projection
a. Optical view
b. Pictorial resemblance view

Plan view

31

Dürer print, modified to show glide-projection demonstration

a. *Picture plane*
b. *Continuous vantage frame*
c. *Lateral armature*
d. *Vantage point sight line*

The Dürer Print: Glide Demonstration

The Dürer print depicting the vase can be set up to demonstrate the principles of glide projection. We shall use the terms described previously in order to describe its general framework.

Glide Actual Projection

Glides, just as perspective, can be conceived in terms of actual and spectator projections. Perspective is based upon point projection, which is the geometry of the single viewing position. Glides are based on the continuous viewing plane, which is the geometry of an infinite number of viewing positions. With so many local station points, chaos and double-imagery problems can easily arise unless they are somehow organized. To prevent double imagery, a lateral armature, here in the form of a point-projective arrangement, organizes the relation between vantage points and lines within the projective field. A complete explanation of the glide-projective structure awaits the following chapter. It is sufficient to say here that the arrangement of lines in the Dürer print demonstrates an actual glide projection.

Glide Spectator Projection

The spectator projection for a glide drawing is based on the mechanical configuration of the eye and is therefore point-projective.

Glide Optical and Pictorial Views

Glides are like decentralized perspectives. As such, there is no one central point from which to view a unified optical glide illusion. Rather, there are many local positions from which to view partial optical views. Each of these local positions is contained on the continuous vantage plane. For the spectator whose eye is located at the position of a vantage point within the glide's continuous vantage plane, there will be at least one line — more than likely, an entire plane — in the viewed illusion that is optically correct. All other lines will be seen in pictorial form, distorted to a greater or lesser extent. As with perspective, distortion exists where bending occurs between spectator and actual projection rays. Thus, glides are generally viewed from completely pictorial spectator positions.

Visual Fields and Viewing Circumstances

The word perspective derives from the Latin term *prospectus,* which means "to look forward." In a sense, that is exactly what we do when we look in perspective, we look forward into space. Glides, on the other hand, glance sideways across the surfaces of things. What are some of the broadest implications of these distinctions? The systems of glide and perspective projections can be interpreted in many different ways. In order to clarify their mutual compatibility, we shall briefly interpret the complementary aspects of each projection system in terms of its visual field and viewing circumstances.

The Perspective Field

The perspective field is a spatial field. This has been understood for centuries. Some believe that the key to the Renaissance rediscovery of perspective was the picture plane, an invisible surface so elusive that it took the entire Middle Ages to slowly recover its meaning. The picture plane is often visualized as a window, and the perspective image is conceived of as the view that is seen through the

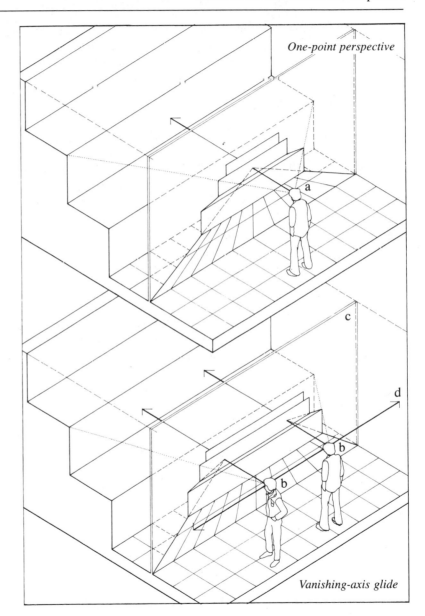

One-point perspective

Vanishing-axis glide

a. *Perspective station point with the full optical view of a spatial field*
b. *Glide vantage point with the partial optical view of an orthogonal plane*
c. *Picture plane*
d. *Continuous vantage axis*

33

window. The idea that the picture plane can be conceived of as a transparent medium, like a window, through which distant spatial prospects can be seen, is consistent with the simplest interpretation of the system of perspective, which asserts that its pictorial image represents objects in space.

The Perspective Viewing Circumstance

If we pause to think about it, the perspective center projective point can be interpreted in two ways. On one hand, the perspective focal point obviously organizes the perspective view; but on the other, this point also exists within the context of its own view. In other words, the focal point is obviously surrounded by the space within which it focuses the perspective view. It is a physical presence, in the form of an optical instrument such as a camera, the human eye, or, more generally, a geometric pencil point, existing somewhere in the middle of a space. Now, the perspective focal point, whether interpreted to represent the eye of a person or the lens of a camera, obviously has the potential to change positions in space, even to move into that which it views in perspective. Other depth clues aside, our eyes focus images in perspective, and perspective enables us to move ahead into the world of our experiences with assurance. Any other projective system would distort this illusion of space. Things close and far would simply not appear as they are. No other system of projection is as effective at interpreting the structure of our view into space.

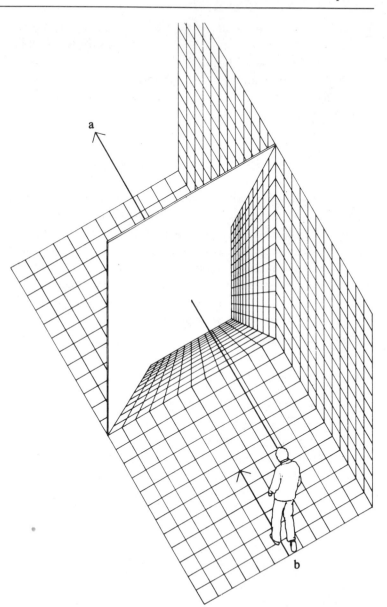

a. *The center of the perspective visual field*
b. *The viewer moves forward into the perspective view*

The Glide Field

The glide visual field and the glide viewing circumstance are different. The perspective field supposes space as the stage for accommodating surfaces. This spatial field is modeled after the way that we see, which in turn is related to the way that we make our way through space. The opposite of the perspective spatial field is the glide surface field, which is interpreted to accommodate spaces.

Surface divides the visual field into two parts: the visually accessible and inaccessible. A good example of a surface that divides the visual field in this way is the ground upon which we walk. The ground is always with us, an imaginary plane that separates our view as we look down at it into that which can be seen and that which is hidden on the other side of its surface.

Now, the unfolding view of a surface is much different than the ongoing view into a space. The view of a surface unfolds laterally, spreading outward and at right angles to its view; the view into space unfolds in depth. Just as there is no limit to the apparent depth of perspective depictions, there are no limits to the apparent breadth of surface views.

The Glide Viewing Circumstance

Because surface views are not intended to be entered into by the viewer, it is absurd to judge a projective system intended for viewing surface contours on the basis of whether or not the viewer can penetrate through the plane of its configuration. Thus, the sort of visual distortion that is undesirable under normal spatial viewing conditions simply does not matter in the view of a surface. The practical value of the projective system used to describe the shape of elements within a surface should therefore be judged solely on the basis of its ability to communicate the outward appearance of its

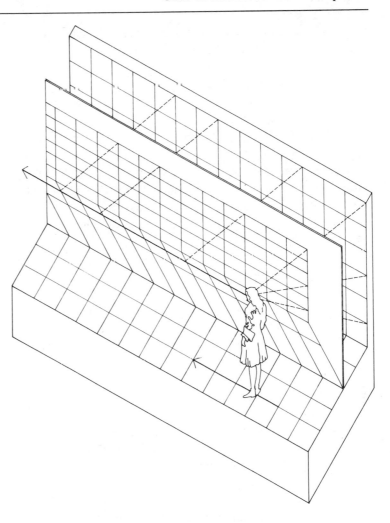

Movement of spectator with respect to the glide projection of a surface

35

contours; it is on the basis of this criterion that glides are more effective than perspectives at depicting surface views.

The separation between the glide spectator and the glide surface has one other effect. As the spectator never enters into the view of the surface, we need not limit the ideal shape of the spectator to that of a point alone. The point can be interpreted as the ideal geometric concept for entering into the center of space, which is a fitting geometrical configuration for the perspective spectator. But, because the glide spectator is circumstantially separated from the plane of the viewed surface, the ideal shape for this spectator is not limited to a point. The glide spectator can therefore be configured in the shape of a line or a plane.

Rules and Methods

It is fitting to end this discussion on theory and interpretation with a few practical observations. In many respects, we value perspective as a pictorial drawing form simply because it works; not only is it capable of structuring the illusion of visual depth, but it is easily learned and constructed as well. The idea that the worth of a system such as perspective can be judged on the merits of its practical consequences alone is based on the pragmatic philosophic tradition, as put forth by philosophers such as William James. We are acting within the bounds of perspective's pragmatic tradition when we ignore its deeper presuppositions in favor of methods for achieving fast and easily constructed visual results.

Perspective has a long and venerable history within this tradition. Alberti's 15th-century treatise, *Della Pittura,* is the oldest book of practical directions on how to construct linear perspectives. His "legitimate construction" method, aimed at painters with no theoretical understanding of perspective principles, laid down simple rules for constructing perspective views. Because of the ease with which perspective rules could be learned and applied, the "legitimate construction" method enjoyed a long period of favor in treatises.

Alberti's method was improved upon in 1505 by J. Pelerin, who used the check for accuracy of the legitimate construction as the method itself, further simplifying the thought process. Pelerin's construction is the ancestor of the well-known distance-point perspective method that is taught in many schools today, a method that generally requires the construction of a gridded spatial box in perspective.

Paralines, under the guise of a perspective view of an infinitely distant object, were brought into the fold of perspective projection in the 17th century. Paralines were, as they are now, a very practical, simple and direct form of pictorial projection.

Glides were never expressed in terms of easily learned and applied methods. Glides were a useful convention during periods in history when graphic modes were inexact, but, Alberti's "legitimate construction" perspective method put an end to the freewheeling use of pictorial effects. The 15th century saw perspective transcend the undisciplined conventions of antiquity. Perspective and its graphic companion, paraline, were transmitted from book to person, or from person to person; glides conventions have not changed much since antiquity. Confined to duties of immediate utility, without easily communicated rules and methods, glides have lapsed into disorderly obscurity, where they have remained until today.

Summary

Renaissance theorists, in accepting the notion of universals, overlooked the thoroughly practical idea that a pictorial illusion is nothing more than an ordering system in the service of particular settings and situations.

The issue as we have discussed it here is not whether there is a contradiction between perspective and glide ordering systems, mere creations of the human mind, but rather how well each system conforms to the real and physical context, to the purposes it is designed to serve. If Renaissance theorists had been willing to let the system conform to the situation rather than the other way around, perhaps glides might have developed into an accepted convention long ago.

Linda Estkowski

The view of an irregular surface

Glide Projection

Introduction

Glide projection, whether accepted as a matter of course or only after critical examination, is the basis for glide drawing. We will learn in another chapter the rules and methods for constructing glide drawings, but for a deeper understanding of glide phenomena, we must consider some basic principles.

Glides, like perspectives, are governed by an internally consistent geometric structure that can be expressed in terms of the conventions of a projective geometry. In theory, glides and perspectives are both capable of structuring views of every conceivable visual situation, from deep spatial corridors to broad and shallow surfaces. However, in practice, the glide view is premised as the complement of the primary perspective view.

When the theorists of the early Renaissance rediscovered the idea of perspective central projection, they could not have realized the influence that the single viewing position would have on the evolu-

tion of pictorial drawing techniques. Long after the success of early demonstrations and treatises on perspective by Brunelleschi and Alberti, other pictorial projective forms were developed, including paralines and ''synthetic'' perspective, yet all the systems had in common that they were structured on the basis of the single viewing position, which implicitly positioned the spectator in the middle of a spatial world.

Perspectives were originally developed to depict the undistorted views of objects in space, from the vantage of persons located within spaces and surrounded by surfaces. Only later were perspectives applied to the birdseye viewpoint, an altogether different viewing experience, meant to be scanned rather than visually penetrated.

Glides, in correcting for the distortion that gradually develops away from the center of broad and shallow perspective delineations, tacitly assume from the beginning that the spectator is not surrounded by space and objects, but rather is located adjacent to a surface that is meant to be visually scanned. On the basis of this different viewing assumption, the geometry of glide projections and the principles governing the way that objects are projected to the surface of a picture plane evolve in a different way.

Glide projection consists of the typical elements of perspective projection — i.e., picture plane, sight line, and viewer — redefined and put together differently in order to form a new projective order. The key element within the glide projective arrangement is the continuous vantage plane, a viewing continuum that parallels the picture plane. On the basis of this concept alone glides are fundamentally different from perspectives. In effect, the vantage plane consists of a multitude of tightly packed and carefully positioned viewing points, all of which glance collectively into the spatial field. It is a plane of many eyes, capable of seeing evenly across sweeping and shallow spaces, a natural counterpoint to the perspective station point, whose single middle viewing location places greater emphasis on happenings toward the center of the spatial field.

There are practical reasons for studying glide projections. Knowing the projective connection between picture and original and understanding differences in projective orders make possible the derivation and classification of drawing types on the basis of their projective qualities. In addition, because a projection expresses a spatial relation between picture and form, conventions and methods for projecting views directly from plan and elevation can be developed.

Our discussion of glide projection begins with a description of the glide visual field, which is followed by a derivation of glide principles, and ends with the conventions of an applied descriptive geometry for glide projections. To ease the task of describing glides, perspectives are used as the model for deriving glide projective relationships.

The View Through the Picture Plane

Before we construct a paraline or perspective drawing, we begin with a blank piece of paper and we imagine, whether we are aware of it or not, that the white of the paper represents the illusion of an empty volume of space. Into this space we introduce figures and surfaces such as buildings and ground planes. When we have completed the drawing, the view looks as if it represents something deep and three-dimensional, as if existing in the space beneath the plane of the paper, as if the paper were a glass window with a view into a miniature world of space and form beyond.

An equally plausible assumption regarding the meaning of the blank paper before us is that it represents the view of a clean, white and smooth surface through which we cannot see. In fact, we can interpret the blankness of the paper as a picture window resting flush upon the surface of a smooth, solid and visually impenetrable substance, such as concrete or stone. Into the plane of the surface of this substance we introduce the shallow three-dimensional images of elements in relief; the features of cityscapes and site plans, the features of any view of the world that is backed by a continuously opaque plane. When the drawing is completed, it conveys the impression of immense breadth of field, with all of its elements protruding or receding as if embossed within the surface of the paper.

Before even one line is introduced into the drawing, we must have an idea of what the blank page before us represents. In this regard, we may assume that the drawing surface itself always represents a transparent picture plane. It is the sameness that we see as we look through the picture plane that can be imagined as either empty space or smooth surface. The view into space or the view of a surface, the only two ways of interpreting the meaning of an empty pictorial field, are the two settings that we may imagine for our blank piece of paper.

Receding Gridded Planes

Spatial and surface visual fields can be constructed on the blank piece of paper. The illusion of a spatial field, which resembles a tunnel, and of a shallow surface field are illustrated at right with gridded planes that appear to recede into depth at right angles to the surface of this page. Observe that the grids defining the surfaces of the receding planes in both views are made up of transverse and orthogonal lines. Transverse grid lines parallel the surface of the drawing paper; orthogonal grid lines recede into depth.

Spatial pictorial illusions like the tunnel field are generally described with either perspective or paraline arrangements of transverse and orthogonal grid lines. Perspective orthogonal receding grids consist of orthogonal grid lines meeting at a point. Their transverse grid lines are spaced in diminishing intervals to converge at the same point. On the other hand, paraline receding orthogonal grids consist of parallel orthogonals and parallel transversals spaced at equal intervals.

Perspective and paraline receding grid patterns are truly useful in situations in which they can be seen to matter. Obviously, deep space is the ideal medium for viewing their effects. But in pictures in which the surface assumes greater importance than the overall depth of field, in which there are no prospects to the sky, no openings to the perspective infinity, in which deep space is walled off or masked from view, and in which the depth of field is very shallow, the conditions are more forgiving and other planar grid patterns are conceivable.

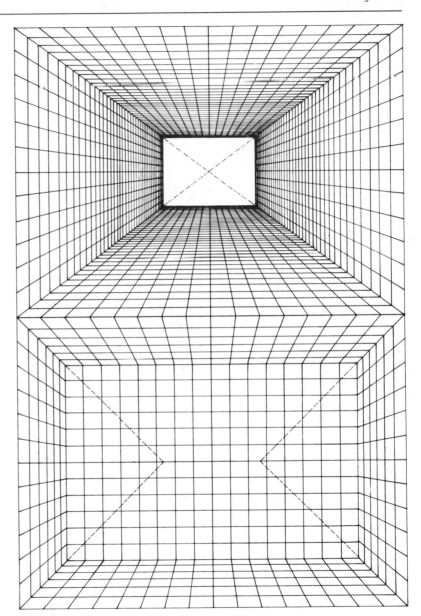

(above) A spatial tunnel defined with perspective orthogonal grids
(below) A shallow surface defined with glide orthogonal grids

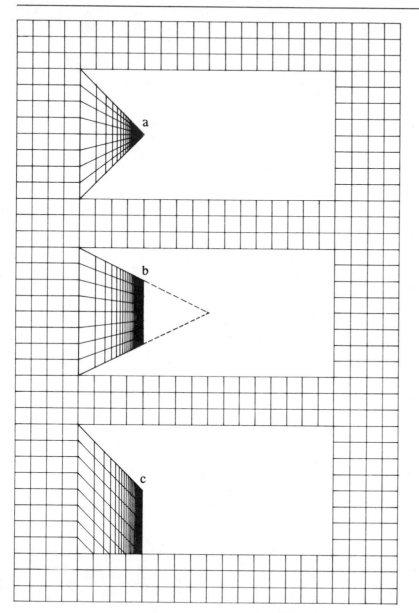

In essence, because they are interpreted as surface projections, glides are not limited to paraline and perspective planar convergence patterns. Glides may include other kinds of receding orthogonal grids. For example, in the shallow spatial construction illustrated on the previous page, two different kinds of receding grids were used to suggest the shallow depth of field. It was not necessary for the receding orthogonals in every plane to meet at a common point in the pictorial view because the distorted pattern of their convergence in deep space was masked behind an opaque transverse shallow surface.

Three of the typical patterns of planar recession that are possible in shallow spatial constructions are illustrated at left. They are point, line, and parallel planar receding grids. Patterns such as these can be put together in many different ways to form different three-dimensional grid configurations, each a different glide visual field.

Receding grids with spatially distorted orthogonal and transverse convergence patterns can be used as pictorial effects in illusions in which their distortion, which increases with depth of field, is masked from view by opaque transverse surface planes. Under these conditions, a system of glide projective geometry can be justified. To describe this system, we shall begin by analyzing pictorial convergence effects in more detail.

Pictorial Convergence Effects

Pictorial convergence can be defined as the meeting of related parallels in the distance of the pictorial illusion. In the case of

a. Orthogonal and transverse grid lines meet at point
b. Transversals diminish to infinity before orthogonals meet at point
c. Transversals diminish to infinity line; orthogonals remain parallel

perspectives, convergence is the meeting of parallels at a point. However, in the case of glide drawings, these parallels could just as easily meet along a line or within a plane.

Since the perspective definition of convergence is not broad enough to include glide vanishing patterns, we must somehow define a general convergence that will admit of line and plane vanishing effects as well. This can be done by separating perspective convergence into two independent parts: lateral and depth.

Imagine the typical perspective scene that shows railroad tracks vanishing to the horizon. The center vanishing point in this view defines both a meeting point for the orthogonal railroad tracks and a limit that cannot be exceeded for the depth intervals between the transverse railroad ties. Perspective illusions of this sort actually show two kinds of convergence occurring at once. The perspective vanishing point defines the limits of depth and lateral convergence simultaneously.

To visualize their separation, consider the same arrangement of railroad tracks and ties, this time with independent convergence limits for depth and for lateral effects. In this case, the railroad ties appear to diminish to infinity before the tracks appear to meet at a point. Although this arrangement contradicts the meaning of true point perspective convergence, it nonetheless remains structurally true that the two phenomena can be expressed independently.

As we shall see, this analysis of normal point perspective convergence into depth and lateral components is ultimately what makes it possible for us to develop our glide projective theory.

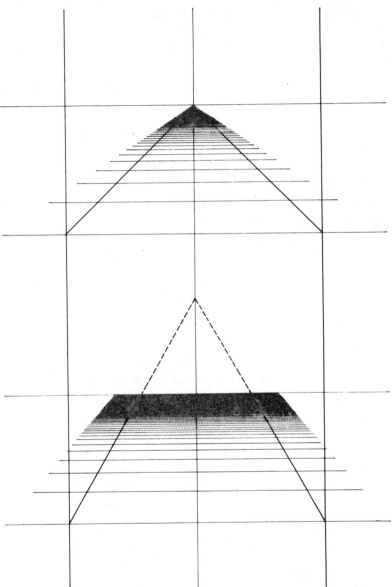

(above) Railroad tracks and ties both meet at perspective vanishing point (below) Railroad ties diminish to an infinity limit before tracks converge to a common point

Lateral and Depth Pictorial Convergence

Perspective convergence, which we shall call unity convergence, can be broken down into two independent parts: lateral and depth convergence. Unity convergence is perspective convergence as we know it.

Of the three convergent forms, by far the simplest to understand, with the most compelling visual properties, even as it challenges our deeper intuition regarding the meaning of convergence, is lateral convergence. Lateral convergence, the shallow component of unity convergence, describes only the convergence patterns of parallels as they occur within the plane of the drawing surface. There is no depth associated with this convergent form. Essentially, lateral convergence coordinates the flat pattern arrangements of parallels within the surface of the pictorial illusion.

Depth convergence, at right angles to lateral convergence, is the projective component of unified convergence. It is projective in the sense that it tells us something about the relative depth of the receding parallel. It is convergent in the sense that the projection of a receding parallel converges in the distance of the pictorial illusion to an infinity plane, just as perspective parallels appear to converge in the distance to a vanishing point that is located on an infinity plane.

Projective Convergence

In order to describe the projective properties that are associated with glide pictorial effects, we shall first take apart perspective projection

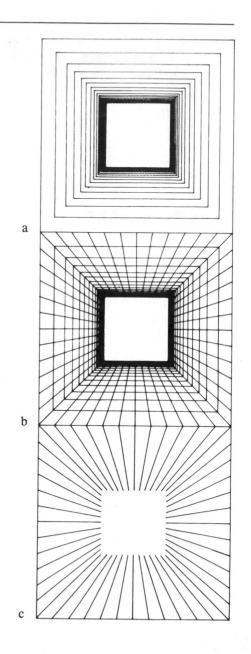

a. Depth convergence lines
b. Unified perspective convergence grid
c. Lateral convergence lines

44

and then put the pieces back together again. Let us begin with a brief review of perspective projection.

We should be familiar with the fact that every perspective image is point-projective and that this image is always recorded on the surface of a picture plane. Of interest to us here is the perspective method by which the vanishing point for related parallels is located on the picture plane.

The general rule of thumb for finding the vanishing point for a set of parallel field lines is to construct a line through the station point, parallel to the set of field lines in question, marking this line's intersection with the picture plane. Under the right conditions, assuming that the parallels in question are also parallel to the ground plane, this rule can be observed to work in the plan view of the perspective as well. In the plan view, the picture plane appears as a line in edge view.

Because of the ease with which the vanishing-point rule can be discussed in plan view, and because effects observed in plan are general enough to apply to all orientations of lines in space, we shall confine our study of perspective and glide convergence phenomena to the plan view only, using station point, edge view of picture plane, sight lines, and field lines as our vocabulary of elements.

Returning to the perspective plan view, the rule for finding the location of the vanishing point along the edge view of the picture plane is actually a description of unified perspective convergence

a. *Picture plane*
b. *Station point*
c. *Parallel field lines*
d. *Line through station point paralleling field lines*
e. *Horizon line*
f. *Vanishing point*
g. *Sight line*

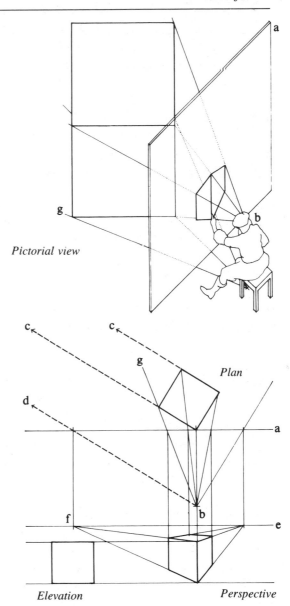

Pictorial view

Plan

Elevation   *Perspective*

stated in projective terms. By definition, parallel field lines converge towards a common point in the perspective image, and this point is the end view of the sight line paralleling the field lines in question.

It is worth pausing here momentarily to describe what we are about to do in order to arrive at our glide projective model. First, we are going to define an elementary vanishing frame, which is the basic building block of every glide variation. Then, we are going to study the behavior of this frame. On the basis of its behavior, we shall relate it with other vanishing frames, and collectively, depending upon how they are arranged, we shall be able to project glide drawings from plan and elevation, as in the office-method perspective.

The Vanishing Frame

The vanishing frame is the elementary glide projective unit. It is the basic building block of every glide projective variation. In essence, the vanishing frame, which is patterned after the perspective rule for locating vanishing points, consists of only one field line and only one paralleling sight line. No more and no less than this.

Because this unit is so basic, the names that are assigned to its various parts are different from those normally associated with the same parts in perspective. Thus, the perspective station point is here referred to as a vantage point. The difference between the two names is only a matter of number. As was mentioned earlier, the station point defines the relation between one paralleling sight line and many field lines; the vanishing frame limits this description to only one field line and one vantage point.

For similar reasons, the perspective vanishing point is here called an infinity point. The infinity point, which is like a local vanishing

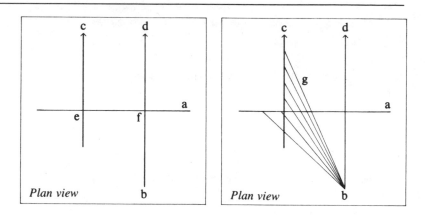

The vanishing frame

a. Picture plane
b. Vantage point
c. Orthogonal field line
d. Paralleling sight line
e. True image point
f. Infinity point
g. Sight line

point, is the point on the surface of the picture plane where the image of one field line appears to vanish — not many field lines, as would be the case in perspective.

With the exception of the different names, the vanishing frame works just as in perspective. Within every vanishing frame, the image of the field line appears to converge towards the paralleling sight line's intersection with the picture plane. This point of intersection is called the infinity point.

These basic vanishing frames can be combined or separated in different ways. For example, when many vanishing frames share a common paralleling sight line, they add up to a normal perspective vanishing structure. When this happens, when overlapping infinity points add to a vanishing point and overlapping vantage points collect at a common station point, then we have a normal perspective projection.

But it is conceivable that all parallel field lines do not share the same paralleling sight line. Remember, perspective convergence is the relation between one sight line and many paralleling field lines; the vanishing frame defines the relation between only one field line and its paralleling sight line. For this reason, our definition of vanishing frame admits of the possibility that there may be more than one station point, or vantage point, from which to view the same pictorial image. For example, there could be two vantage points, each paired with a separate field line. Each of the parallel field lines would therefore appear to vanish towards a different point in the pictorial view.

Given this basic vanishing frame, our task is to bring order to situations in which the vanishing frames do not all share a common paralleling sight line, which is to bring order to the glide view. One

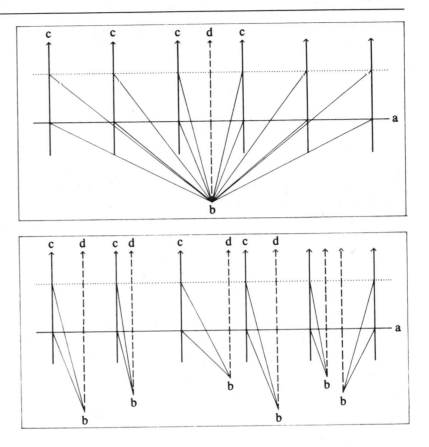

a. Picture plane
b. Vantage point
c. Orthogonal field line
d. Paralleling sight line

47

more thing should be mentioned before moving on to an analysis of the vanishing frame. For reasons explained at the end of this chapter, we shall assume that all field lines orient orthogonally, or at right angles to the picture plane.

Foreshortening and Diminution

For the sake of simplicity, we shall assume that all field lines begin at the surface of the picture plane and extend to infinity. Thus, within a vanishing frame, the sighted image of a field line begins at its intersection with the picture plane, called its true image point, and ends at its infinity point. Given this basic structure, it is obvious that the image of a field line, or image line, will vary depending upon the position of the vantage point. For example, if the vantage point is shifted further away from the field line, then the image of the field line, or image line, will be longer.

Depending upon how we move the vantage point with respect to the field line, we can change the degree of foreshortening or the rate of diminution of its projected image. In particular, transverse movement, which is movement paralleling the picture plane, affects the degree of foreshortening of the image line, while orthogonal movement, which is movement at right angles to the picture plane, affects the rate of diminution of the image line. The two vantage-point movements, transverse and orthogonal, are independent.

Before we proceed any further, it is important to understand what we are about to explain. Although the effects of foreshortening and diminution can be verified in the abstract with the aid of definitions and theorems, we are only interested in grasping the gist of the idea here. We shall therefore present examples that demonstrate the independence of transverse and orthogonal movements without proving this independence.

a. *Picture plane*
b. *Vantage point*
c. *Orthogonal field line*
d. *Paralleling sight line*
e. *True image point*
f. *Infinity point*

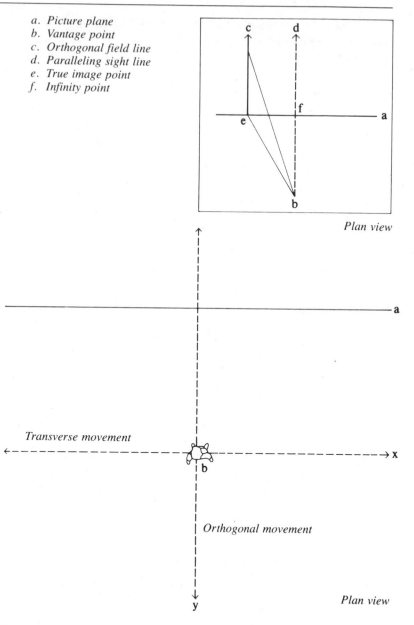

Plan view

Transverse movement

Orthogonal movement

Plan view

Imagine a vanishing structure that includes one unique sight line. This sight line is special because the projected image of the point that it sights along the field line just happens to divide the total length of the image line into two equal parts. Let's call this particular setup our reference vanishing frame.

Observe what happens when the vantage point for this reference frame is shifted transversely. The image line becomes longer, yet its unique sight line still divides the total length of its projected image into two equal parts. When this happens, the foreshortened length of the projected field line varies, yet the rate of diminution of its parts remains constant.

With transverse movement, the total length of the projected image of the field line, measured from its image point to its infinity point on the surface of the picture plane, becomes longer. This suggests that the image of the field line is less foreshortened. Yet, the uniquely sighted depth of the field line bisects the total image length of the field line in both views. This suggests that the length of a projected interval along the field line is proportional to the total length of the projected field interval, regardless of the transverse location of the vantage point. In this case, the ratio is 1:2 in both views of the field line. The rate of diminution for the projected image of the field line does not change with transverse movement of the vantage point.

Diminution is difficult to understand. To further visualize what is meant by rate of diminution, recall the railroad-track example. In this example, depth convergence was related to the spacing of the railroad ties. It was related to the diminishing intervals between these ties as they vanished towards the horizon line. Depth convergence is measured as rate of diminution, in terms of how fast intervals appear to decrease as they move into the distance. In all

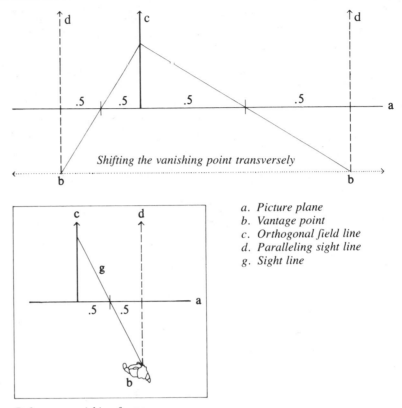

Shifting the vanishing point transversely

Reference vanishing frame

a. *Picture plane*
b. *Vantage point*
c. *Orthogonal field line*
d. *Paralleling sight line*
g. *Sight line*

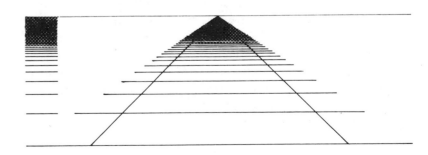

cases, the rate of diminution of vanishing field lines is preserved when the ratio of their depth intervals to the total length of their projected image is the same.

Orthogonal movement of the vantage point, on the other hand, has the opposite effect of transverse movement. With this movement, although the total length of the projected image line will remain the same, the rate at which its projected intervals appear to vanish will vary. Moving the vantage point orthogonally does not affect the foreshortened length of the image line, but it does change its rate of diminution.

Let's look at a one-point perspective example. Suppose that we construct the silhouette of a simple gabled house and then project that silhouette to a common vanishing point in the distance. Observe that by dividing every projector line in half and then connecting these points, we arrive at a replica shape of the original silhouette, only smaller in size. This, of course, is a one-point perspective construction.

It just so happens that in every one-point perspective construction, the rate of diminution for all vanishing orthogonals within the visual field remains constant. Only the degree of foreshortening of their image lines varies. This is true because for every orthogonal field line, the perspective station point is obviously located at the same distance from the picture plane. What varies between station point and field line is the transverse or lateral distance separating the two. One-point perspective foreshortening and diminution effects are the same as those that occur within reference-vanishing-frame setups. One thing is different. Rather than hold the field line constant while varying the location of the vantage point, the one-point-perspective setup holds the position of the station point constant while varying the location of the field line.

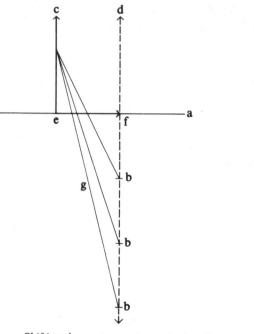

a. *Picture plane*
b. *Vantage point*
c. *Orthogonal field line*
d. *Paralleling sight line*
e. *True image point*
f. *Infinity point*
g. *Sight line*

Shifting the vantage point orthogonally

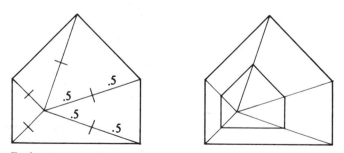

Each orthogonal line is divided in half

Suppose that the position of the central vanishing point is shifted to a new location. Within the perspective view, if each of the vanishing orthogonals is again divided in half to suggest a common depth interval and these points are connected, we again obtain a shape replica of the original silhouette. This is a one-point view of the same house as seen from a different station point. It can be assumed that the station points for both constructions are located at the same distance from the picture plane because the rate of diminution for orthogonal lines is the same in both views.

Now, suppose that the house's five receding orthogonals vanish toward different infinity points, not just one. If each of these lines is divided in half to suggest a common depth, it can be assumed that the individual vantage points for each of these orthogonals are located at the same distance from the picture plane because the rate of diminution for each line is the same. It can further be assumed that each of the individual vantage points for each of the individual vanishing orthogonals is positioned along the orthogonal sight line that defines the infinity point for each of the vanishing orthogonals. In effect, in this last example, we have dissolved the central perspective station point into five individual vantage points, each of which is located at the same distance from the picture plane. Because these vantage points all lie within a common plane that parallels the picture plane, the rate of diminution of their field lines must be the same. What varies, and what we shall have to concern ourselves with next, is the foreshortened length and direction for each separate field line.

The Glide Projective Assembly

So far, we have analyzed the elements of typical perspective phenomena. In order to define glide projective geometry, we shall put these elements together again in a slightly new way.

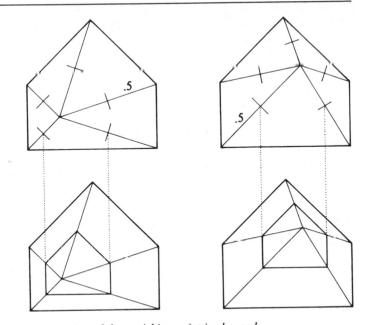

The position of the vanishing point is changed

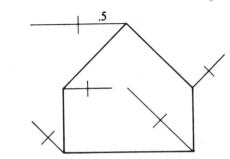

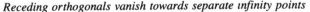

Receding orthogonals vanish towards separate infinity points

51

The basic elements of every glide projection include: the picture plane, the vanishing frame, the continuous vantage plane, the lateral armature, and the visual field.

With the exception of the picture plane, all these elements are different than those that we normally associate with perspective. One that may appear to be the same as in perspective but in fact is quite different is the glide visual field. Before we discuss the rules for putting together a glide projection, let's first understand the nature of this visual field.

The Glide Visual Field

Unlike the perspective visual field, where lines are free to travel in every direction, the glide field is made up of only one set of parallel lines. The glide field can be imagined as an enormous bundle of individual fibers, all packed closely together. Each of these fibers is the equivalent of one field line. All are parallel to each other and, for reasons that are explained later, perpendicular to the picture plane. Every fiber is like a miniature visual field because each has its own vantage point and sight lines, and each fiber, or field line, projects to the surface of the picture plane in accordance with the vanishing frame that is assigned to it.

Thus, the glide field is actually composed of many closely packed yet independent field lines, all parallel to each other and perpendicu-

a. *Picture plane*
b. *Vantage point*
c. *Orthogonal field line*
d. *Paralleling sight line*
e. *True image point*
f. *Infinity point*
h. *Continuous vantage plane*
i. *Lateral armature*

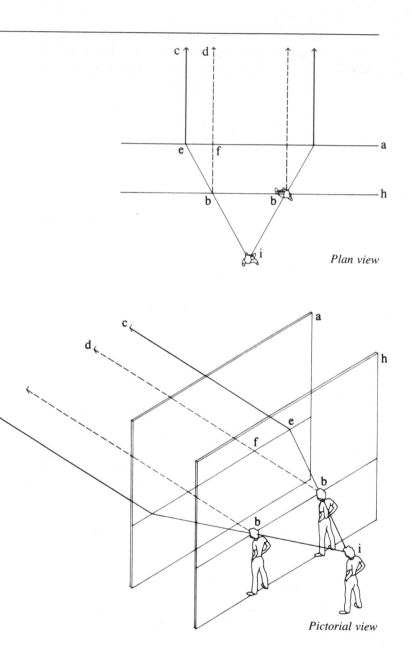

Plan view

Pictorial view

52

lar to the picture plane. It is necessary for us to structure the glide visual field in this unusual and restrictive way in order to make it possible for us to consider multiple viewing points.

When the glide field is ordered into a bundle of parallel field lines, we are able to conceive of as many different vantage positions, or station points, as there are lines in the visual field.

By definition, we shall therefore agree that every field line within the glide visual field is paired with one vanishing frame. Each of these vanishing frames consists of one vantage point, one paralleling sight line, one infinity point, and one field line. Each frame is, in essence, a very specialized perspective of one line in space.

We have defined the bundled glide field. We have also paired each of its field lines with one vanishing frame. The bundled field, the vanishing frame, and the picture plane are the central pieces of our glide arrangement. Yet one feature is still missing: there is no order to the position of the vantage points, and hence there can be no order to the projected pictorial image. As we shall see, vantage points are ordered with two important glide elements: the continuous vantage plane, which regulates pictorial diminution, and the lateral armature, which regulates lateral convergence effects.

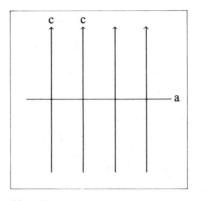

Plan view

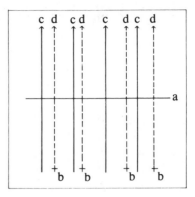

Plan view

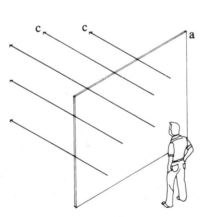

Pictorial view

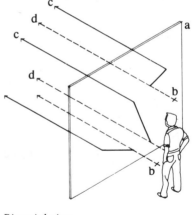

Pictorial view

a. *Picture plane*
b. *Vantage point*
c. *Orthogonal field line*
d. *Paralleling sight line*

53

The Continuous Vantage Plane

By definition, this plane parallels the picture plane and contains all vantage points. The continuous vantage plane controls the rate of diminution for all lines within the glide visual field.

To grasp the need for the continuous vantage plane, recall that every vantage point belongs to a basic vanishing-frame structure and that within every vanishing-frame structure, transverse movement of the vantage point with respect to the picture plane will affect the degree of foreshortening of the projected image of a field line but not its rate of diminution. Thus, if all vantage points for all vanishing frames are conveniently located within the same transverse plane, here called the continuous vantage plane, we can be certain that no matter how vantage points are situated with respect to their field lines, the rate of diminution for their projected images will be the same. The continuous vantage plane ultimately controls pictorial convergence in depth.

The Lateral Armature

The other important regulating element is the lateral armature, which ultimately controls the degree of foreshortening for all field lines within the glide projective image. In essence, it is an ordering system that coordinates the pairing of field lines with vantage points, thus regulating the overall unity of lateral convergence effects. As we shall see, the shape of the lateral armature can vary, and it is the differences in its patterns that enable us to conceive of alternative forms of glide projection.

Every projective lateral armature consists of three important parts:

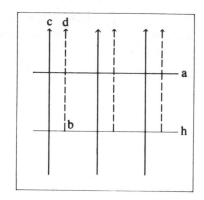

Plan view

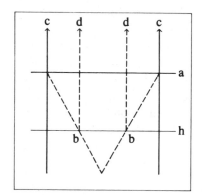

Plan view

a. Picture plane
b. Vantage point
c. Orthogonal field line
d. Paralleling sight line
h. Continuous vantage plane

its staging rectangle, its four staging orthogonals, and its staging projectors. All these elements combine to form the template or recipe for constructing the lateral convergence of vanishing orthogonals within the pictorial view. The armature itself can be likened to a skeleton or framework that suggests the order of the relation between vantage points and field lines.

Double-imagery Rule

In order to assure the uniqueness of the glide projected image, the lateral armature must pair vantage points with field lines so as not to violate the double-imagery rule. In other words, no individual point in the glide visual field should project to the picture plane in more than one location. If we agree to accept as a rule that every field line may have one and only one vantage point, there will be no problem with double imagery.

The reason for stating the rule in this way is obvious. Every point in the glide visual field belongs to only one field line, and this unique field line is in turn associated with only one vantage point. The projected image of this point in space can only be sighted from the vantage point that is paired with its field line, and hence its image cannot occur in more than one place on the picture plane.

How shall we actually pair each field line with its individual vantage point? We shall agree that the one-to-one correspondence between vantage point and field line can be made with a straight-line connection between the vantage point and the true image point of the field line. These true image points are always contained on the picture plane.

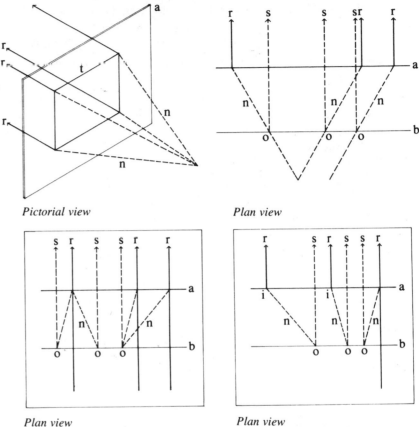

Pictorial view

Plan view

Plan view

Plan view

a. *Picture plane*
b. *Continuous vantage plane*
i. *True image point*
n. *Connector lines*
o. *Vantage points*
r. *Orthogonal field line*
s. *Paralleling sight line*
t. *Staging rectangle*

Straight-line connectors are called staging projectors if they are a part of the lateral armature. Every three-dimensional lateral armature consists of a total of four of these staging projectors. If straight-line connectors are not staging projectors, then we shall simply call them connectors, or connector lines. As we shall see, once the order of the four staging connectors is established, all the other connectors can be constructed on the basis of their staging pattern.

Image-continuity Rule

In addition to the double-imagery rule, the lateral armature must also obey the image-continuity rule. This rule is intended to eliminate the possibility of creating undefined spaces within the glide pictorial image. Undefined spaces are like the undesirable voids that exist in the middle of split paraline pictorial constructions.

To avoid undefined spaces within the glide pictorial view, the continuity rule states that the patterned configuration of the lateral armature must not contain gaps between adjacent vantage points on the continuous vantage plane. In other words, the lateral armature itself must set the stage for defining a continuous plane of vantage points.

Provided the double-imagery and image-continuity rules stated above are not broken, the lateral armature can assume many different geometric configurations. Each configuration defines a unique pattern of lateral convergence within a glide pictorial illusion.

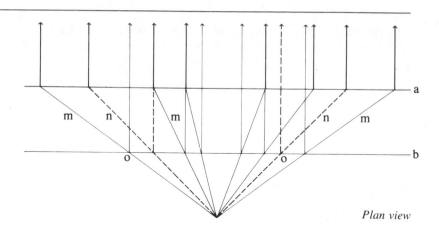

Plan view

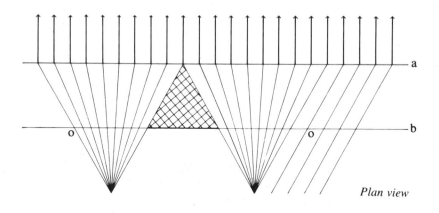

Plan view

a. Picture plane
b. Continuous vantage plane
m. Staging projector
n. Connector line
o. Vantage point

The gridded area projects as a gap on the continuous vantage plane

56

Two Basic Lateral Armatures

In order to develop a feeling for the glide projective mechanism, let's look at a few simple planar lateral armatures. These examples are patterned after the office-method perspective-plan arrangement.

Imagine the section view through a shallow rectangular space whose interior is divided into three separate cells by two walls. A picture plane, seen in edge view, cuts through the front edge of this space in the section view. A continuous vantage plane, also seen in edge view, is positioned behind the picture plane.

In this section view, the walls of the shallow rectangular space are seen as orthographic field lines, which intersect the picture plane at four separate true image points. The true image points for these field lines can be paired with vantage points on the continuous vantage plane in several different ways. Depending upon the order, a different glide-drawing variation will ensue.

For example, if we order the relation between vantage points and image points with a point-projective lateral armature, then the lines radiating from its central focus to the true image points on the picture plane will cross the continuous vantage plane at four different locations. Each of these locations marks the position of a vantage point for each of the four field lines. Once the order between vantage points and field lines has been established, every vantage-point-field-line relation can be treated as a separate vanishing frame, which means that the image of a point along a field line can be sighted from the field line's respective vantage point. This process is really no different than the one-point office method, which locates

a. *Picture plane*
b. *Continuous vantage plane*
m. *Staging projector*
n. *Connector line*

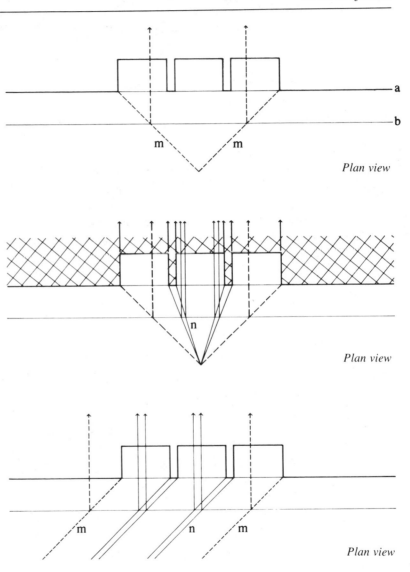

Plan view

Plan view

Plan view

the images of points in space from a single station point rather than many individual vantage positions.

The point-projective lateral armature is not the only conceivable geometry for ordering the relation between field lines and vantage points. For instance, the lateral armature could also be ordered with parallel connectors. With this arrangement, every true image point would be paired with its vantage point by parallel oblique projection. The same process of using the vanishing frame to project the images of individual points along field lines would again be applied.

Perspective images can be constructed from plan and elevation views. The same holds true of glide drawings. The method that we shall use to project glide images directly from plan and elevation views is similar to the one-point office method for projecting perspectives. Just as with the office method, the edge view of the picture plane appears in top and side elevation, and its frontal view appears in the area where the glide image is constructed. By convention, we shall only be dealing with surface, or shallow spatial constructions. By convention, we shall also cut the picture plane through the most important plane of the surface depicted. In most cases the picture plane is positioned so that it is contained within the forward plane of the surface.

The shallow space that was illustrated in plan only on the previous page is here shown as a glide view projected from top and side views. Let's review the step-by-step procedure for constructing glide images in this way. The setup is straightforward. In this case the comparatively shallow depth of the space is shown in both top

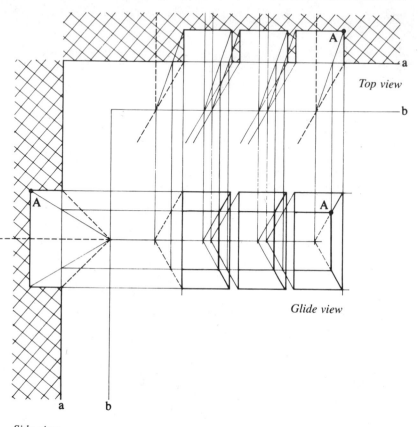

Top view

Glide view

Side view

a. *Picture plane*
b. *Continuous vantage plane*

and side views. A plan layout of the space is shown in the frontal view.

The edge view of the picture plane is constructed in top and side views, and the edge view of the continuous vantage plane is included in both views. The continuous vantage plane can be located at any distance from the picture plane, provided that this distance is the same in both views.

A lateral armature for ordering the relation between the image points for field lines and their respective vantage points on the continuous vantage plane is introduced. In the example a planar parallel armature was used to order this relation in top view, and a planar point-convergent armature was selected for the side view. The reason for varying the pattern of the armature in these two views will be explained later. Here it is only important to note that the point and parallel armatures order one and only one vantage point for every image point in both views.

After the location of the vantage points has been established, the actual projection can begin. Each vantage-point-image-point pairing is a vanishing frame. Thus, the projected depth of every point on every field line can be sighted from the vantage point that is paired with its respective field line. This is done in much the same way that images are projected to the surface of the picture plane in perspective. The only difference between projecting images in perspective and projecting images in glide is that perspectives have only one vantage point from which to sight all points and lines in space, while glides have many vantage points. It is therefore important to project the image of every point in the glide visual field only from the vantage point that is associated with the point's field line.

Let us pause briefly here to remember that we are constructing this glide projection as a three-view drawing. For this reason, the same point in the glide visual field will appear once in each of the three views: frontal, top, and side. By convention, each real point in the visual field can be assigned a letter, such as A, B, or C. The image of one real point in the visual field will thus be labeled with a letter in each of the three views.

The image of any point, A, as it will appear in the frontal glide pictorial view, can be found by sighting the point's intersection with the edge view of the picture plane in both top and side views. To do this, the point's vanishing frame, which includes the point's unique vantage position, is used to determine its projected position along the edge view of the picture plane in both top and side views. The image of the point in the frontal view can be found by transferring its intersections with the picture plane orthogonally into the frontal view. The point where these transferred lines meet in the frontal view marks the location of point A in the glide pictorial image.

The same process can be repeated for every point in the glide projective field. After enough points have been projected into the frontal view, they can be connected together to form the completed projective image.

Four Planar Lateral Armatures

The lateral armature brings order to the relation between orthogonal field lines and vantage points. In two dimensions this order can be defined with a minimum of two staging connector lines. Together, these lines form a planar lateral armature. We can construct the relation between all image points and vantage points on the basis of the pattern of these two lines.

So far, we have considered two ways in which to order the two-dimensional, or planar, relation between image points and vantage points. We called them line and parallel lateral armatures. But there are other ways to order this relation, four of which are useful for depicting glide pictorial views. These four patterns we shall call point, line, parallel, and diverging planar lateral armatures.

Every one of these armatures can be expressed with a minimum of two lines and every one suggests the pattern for relating individual image points on the picture plane with particular vantage points on the continuous vantage plane.

Two of the four patterns deserve brief explanations because of their unusual properties. First of all, the point pattern relates all true image points to only one vantage point on the continuous vantage plane. This relation would appear to be similar to the relation between perspective field lines and the single station point. But there is a subtle difference. The configuration of the glide one-point visual field resembles a tube, whereas the perspective visual field is structured to resemble an ever-expanding pyramid of vision.

The diverging lateral armature is also unusual in that it makes possible the construction of inverse perspective effects — that is, effects in which objects within the visual field appear to grow larger

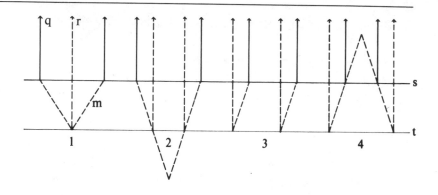

1. *Point planar lateral armature*
2. *Line planar lateral armature*
3. *Parallel planar lateral armature*
4. *Diverging planar lateral armature*

Plan view

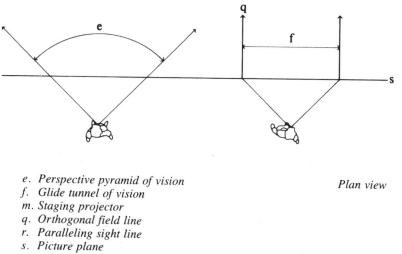

e. *Perspective pyramid of vision*
f. *Glide tunnel of vision*
m. *Staging projector*
q. *Orthogonal field line*
r. *Paralleling sight line*
s. *Picture plane*
t. *Continuous vantage plane*

Plan view

as they recede into the distance. While this lateral armature may not be useful in itself, it is quite practical when combined with other armatures.

Six Core and Four Diverging Three-dimensional Armatures

The four two-dimensional planar armatures can be combined to form three-dimensional armatures. One such combination was described earlier in the example of the glide image that was projected from top and side views. Recall that the top view was a parallel armature and the side view a line armature. Together, they formed a keystone glide, which is based on a keystone armature, the name given to the three-dimensional armature that is a cross between the line and the parallel planar armature.

The six core three-dimensional armatures are made up of combinations of point, line, and parallel lateral frames. The spatial configuration for these core armatures is shown at right. Each has a special name. There are vanishing-point, vanishing-axis, vanishing-plane, herringbone, keystone, and box armature variations within the core group.

In addition to the core lateral armatures are the diverging frames. These are called point-diverging, plane-diverging, parallel-diverging, and inverse-lateral armatures. Although intriguing diverging pictorial effects can be achieved in the glide image, diverging armatures have limited practical applications.

The four diverging armatures
1. Plane diverging
2. Point diverging
3. Parallel diverging
4. Inverse

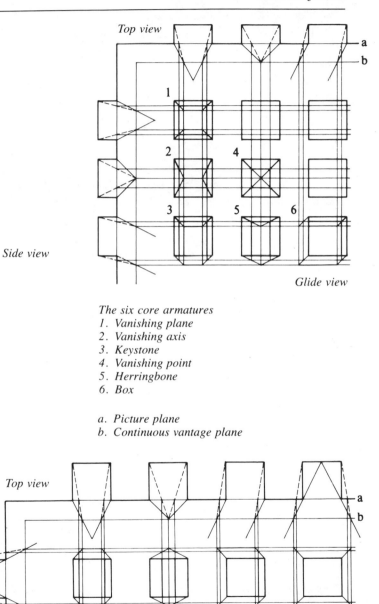

Top view

Side view

Glide view

The six core armatures
1. Vanishing plane
2. Vanishing axis
3. Keystone
4. Vanishing point
5. Herringbone
6. Box

a. Picture plane
b. Continuous vantage plane

Top view

Glide view

Infinity Planes

What is the difference between a herringbone and a keystone lateral armature? The relative position of the infinity plane. This plane, which is a transverse plane, represents the absolute limit of diminution or depth that is attainable within the glide pictorial view. In the case of the keystone armature, the limits of projected depths are reached before vanishing orthogonals reach their lateral convergence points. The keystone lateral armature provides a shallower projective view than the herringbone armature. The difference between the vanishing-point and vanishing-area armatures is solely based on the location of their respective infinity planes.

By convention, solid orthogonal lines within the lateral armature are interpreted to exist on the viewer's side of the infinity plane. Dashed orthogonals, or portions thereof, exist on the other side of the transverse infinity plane.

Selected Projections

For the sake of further clarifying the glide projective process, some three-view examples, complete with construction lines, are included here.

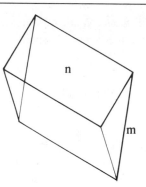

The schematic pattern of convergence for orthogonal lines and planes

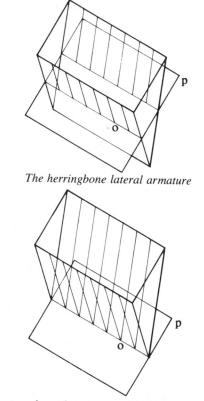

The herringbone lateral armature

n. Staging rectangle
m. Staging orthogonal
o. Infinity point
p. Infinity plane

The keystone lateral armature with shallow infinity plane

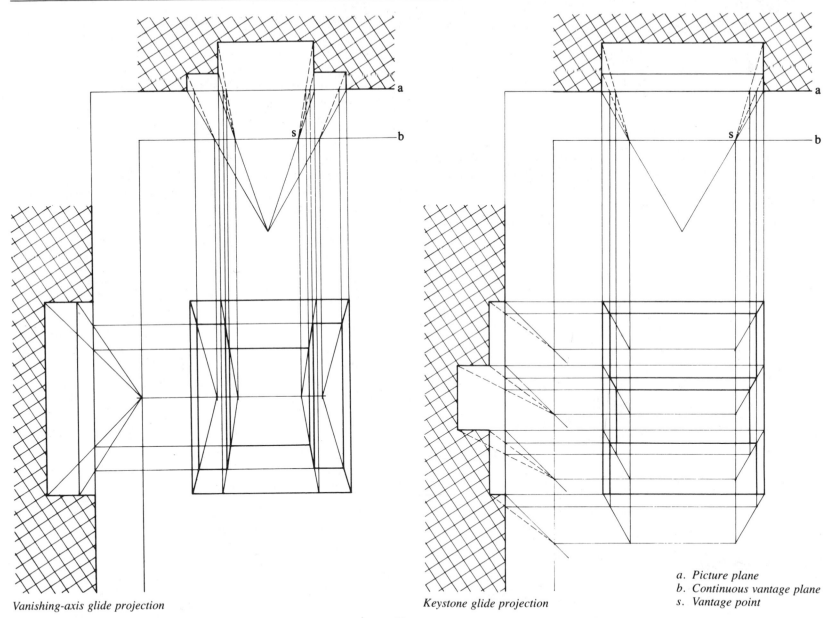

a. Picture plane
b. Continuous vantage plane
s. Vantage point

Vanishing-axis glide projection

Keystone glide projection

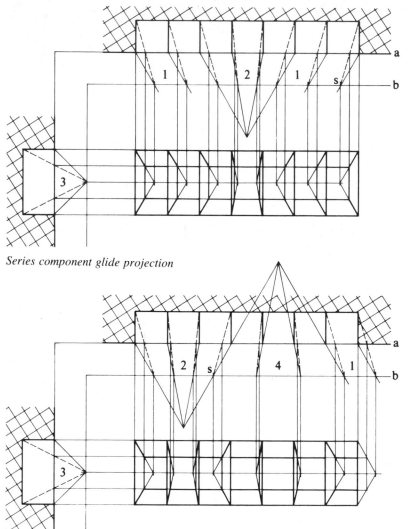

Series component glide projection

Series component glide projection

Component Glide Projections

Obviously, every one of the six core and four diverging lateral armatures can be used independently to structure the relation between all vantage points and field lines within a glide pictorial construction. Not so obvious is the fact that more than one of these armatures can be combined within the same pictorial construction. When more than one armature is used within the same glide construction, it is called a component projection.

The method for projecting a component glide drawing is the same as that for structuring normal glide views. What changes is the configuration of the lateral armature. More than one armature orders the glide projective view. In theory, any combination of core and diverging lateral armatures is permitted within the same construction, provided that the conditions for image continuity and double imagery, mentioned earlier in the chapter, are adhered to.

Examples of component glide configurations are shown at left. Note that no gaps or overlaps exist between adjoining armatures. Note also that in every projection, every field-line image point pairs with only one vantage point. Component glide projections exploit the fact that the foreshortened length and orientation of projected field lines is independent of the rate of diminution of the visual field.

a. *Picture plane*
b. *Continuous vantage plane*
s. *Vantage point*

1. *Parallel planar lateral armature*
2. *Line planar lateral armature*
3. *Point planar lateral armature*
4. *Diverging planar lateral armature*

How to Project a Component Glide Image

The procedure for projecting component glide drawings is the same as that for projecting individual core and diverging pictorial views. We can divide this process into two parts: the setup and the projection. The setup consists of the following:

(1) Construct three views, top, side, and front, of a shallow spatial form.
(2) Introduce a picture plane, seen in edge view, in top and side elevations. This plane should cut through the most significant transverse plane of the shallow space.
(3) Construct a continuous vantage plane parallel to the picture plane. The distance separating the continuous vantage plane from the picture plane is not important. Effects gained by moving the continuous vantage plane closer or further away from the picture plane can be judged on the basis of experiment.
(4) Construct lateral armatures in top and side views. Here we shall use three lateral armatures in the top view and one in the side view. The armatures in the top view consist of a point pattern flanked by two parallel patterns. The armature in the side view is a line pattern. As a rule, every orthogonal field line is associated with its respective vantage point by means of the armature pattern that contains its true image point.

The projection follows from this setup. In both top and side views use vanishing frames to determine the projected depths of points on selected field lines. Transfer projected depths into the pictorial image, connecting related points in order to arrive at the completed glide view. Note that in the pictorial view all orthogonal lines within the boundaries of a particular lateral armature vanish in accordance with its pattern of recession.

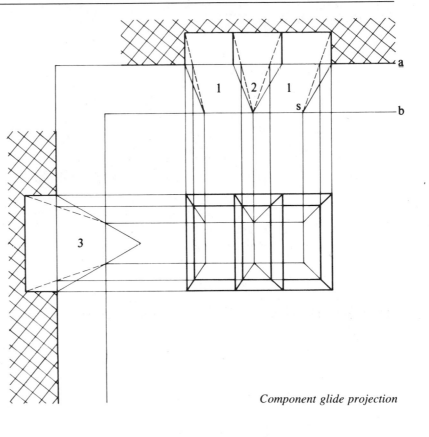

Component glide projection

a. *Picture plane*
b. *Continuous vantage plane*
s. *Vantage point*

1. *Parallel planar armature*
2. *Point planar armature*
3. *Line planar armature*

Core Component Projections

Component glide projections can be divided into two general categories: those that are arranged around a center and those that are arranged along a line. Center arrangements are called core component projections; linear arrangements are called series component glides.

There are three component core variations, each with a different lateral armature in its center. All three of these alternatives divide the glide pictorial field into nine adjoining lateral armatures. The most useful of these core component projections consists of a vanishing-point armature in the center, flanked on its four sides by herringbone armatures, with four box armatures in the corners.

A variation on this core configuration places a vanishing-plane armature in the center. This is flanked by keystone armatures, with box armatures in the corners. The only difference between this core construction and the one with the vanishing-point armature in its center is the position of the infinity plane. Because of this difference, one is shallower than the other.

Vanishing-point and vanishing-plane core component glide constructions are both symmetrical projections, consisting of the same armature on all four sides of the center armature. There is also an asymmetric core configuration, one with two different pairs of armatures adjoining the center armature. This configuration has a vanishing-axis construction in the center, which is flanked by two keystone and two herringbone lateral armatures. Box armatures are at the corners.

These three core component glide projections can be used to structure both square and rectangular surface forms. In fact, the frontal

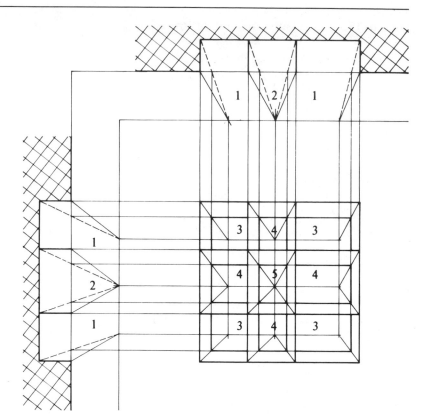

Vanishing-point core component projection

1. Parallel planar armature
2. Point planar armature
3. Box armature
4. Herringbone armature
5. One-point armature

shape of each of the nine individual armatures that make up a core projection can be any rectangular shape, provided no gaps or overlaps occur between their adjacent boundaries. Examples of all three core constructions, presented as three-view projections, are illustrated at right.

Series Component Glides

Series component glides consist of strings of lateral armatures. These strings can be made up of repeating or nonrepeating sequences of armatures.

Nonrepeating-series component glide projections are limited to strings of two or three core lateral armatures. Examples of such strings include the herringbone-vanishing-point-herringbone, the keystone-vanishing-plane-keystone, and the herringbone-vanishing-axis-herringbone sequences. Note that these strings have the same arrangement as that of the lateral armatures through the middle of a core component projection.

Repeating-series component projections make use of diverging lateral armatures. These armatures, mentioned earlier in the chapter, link to the ends of core sequences in order to make the basic repeat pattern for endlessly long series glide projections. At least one of the four basic diverging lateral armatures, named diverging plane, diverging parallel, diverging line and diverging point, connects two related sequences of core constructions. Various combinations of glide repeating-series arrangements are shown at right.

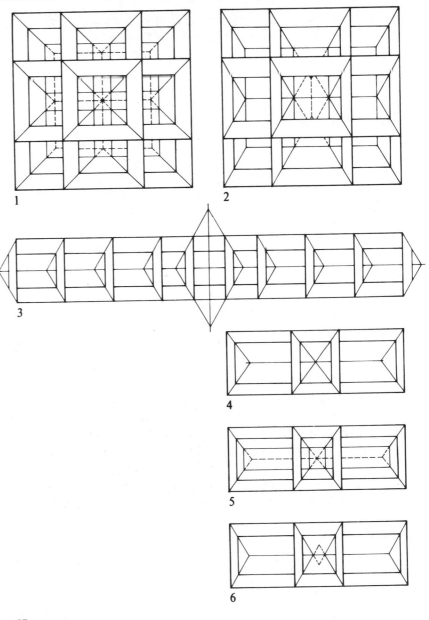

1. Vanishing-plane core component projection
2. Vanishing-axis core component projection
3. Repeating string sequence is possible with diverging armature
4. Herringbone–vanishing point–herringbone series component glide
5. Keystone–vanishing area–keystone series component glide
6. Herringbone–vanishing axis–herringbone series component glide

67

Series arrangements are useful for depicting long and narrow scenes such as shallow relief within street elevations and street plans.

Eccentric Projective Effects

All of the glide projections described so far have depicted gridlike surface forms. But surfaces in the real world often contain nonaxial and oblique lines and planes as well. How do these elements appear within the glide projection? In general, such lines and planes pose no problem, provided that the depth of field of the glide projection is kept shallow, just as the perspective breadth of field must be kept narrow.

One of the reasons for placing this restriction on the glide projective field is to reduce the curvature of certain diagonal and nonaxial lines within the glide projective view. When the space is shallow, the curvature of nonaxial lines is minimal — in fact, hardly noticeable. As the depth of the glide construction increases, the curvature of certain nonaxial lines becomes pronounced.

Here are some observations regarding the behavior of certain nonaxial lines within the glide view. Every orthogonal line will, of course, remain straight. In addition, every straight line within every transverse plane will remain straight, regardless of the depth of projection. However, in many cases the orientation of transverse nonaxial lines will change upon projection. Thus, the image of a diagonal wall within the plan view of a vanishing-axis glide projection will appear to twist as it recedes into depth; yet, every one of the transverse lines that makes up the wall will in itself remain straight. Only the orientation of each of the transverse lines will vary, depending upon the depth of projection.

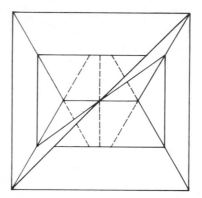

Twisting distortion

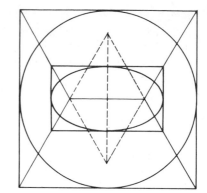

Stretching distortion

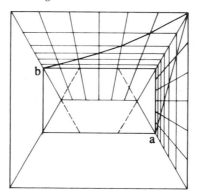

Curving distortion

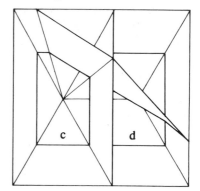

Bending distortion

a. *Straight diagonal*
b. *Curving diagonal*
c. *Vanishing-point armature*
d. *Herringbone armature*

68

Nonorthogonal field lines may or may not remain straight, depending upon the type of vanishing plane in which they are contained. If the plane vanishes towards a point, then all the obliques and diagonals within the plane will remain straight. On the other hand, if the plane vanishes toward a line rather than a point, all the diagonals and obliques within its surface will appear to curve.

Another reason for limiting the glide depth of field is to minimize distortion of the projected images of shapes from one transverse plane to another. This occurs in asymmetrical glide projections such as the vanishing-axis construction. Thus, a grid of squares on the picture plane may project in depth to a grid of rectangles. Obviously, the shallower the projection, the less noticeable the distortion.

Yet another eccentric pictorial effect can be observed in the behavior of nonaxial lines within component glide constructions. Within every transverse plane except the picture plane, these nonaxial lines will appear to bend as they cross the boundaries between lateral armature fields. Again, this distortion can be reduced by keeping the projective field shallow, because the degree of bending increases with the depth of field.

Glide Two-point Projections

It is theoretically possible to construct or project two-point glide images of objects in space. However, for practical reasons these projections make little sense, because at least one of the three principal coordinate axes must curve. Since three coordinate axes typically describe the principal lines of most architectural objects in space, it is a good idea to keep these axes straight in the pictorial construction, because it is far easier to construct lines with a straightedge than it is to connect points together with a french curve.

Why must one of the three coordinate axes within a glide two-point construction appear to curve? Because within the glide illusion, the projected images for only one set of parallel field lines can remain straight. With the exception of the chosen orientation of straight field lines, all other sets of related depth parallels within the glide image will appear to curve. Even though the set of glide field lines that project as straight lines could be chosen to orient obliquely rather than orthogonally with respect to the picture plane, we intentionally choose to project straight orthogonal field lines because it is desirable to have three axes in the glide visual field project as straight lines. Two of these axes must be contained within transverse planes. If three coordinate axes are to remain straight within the glide construction, the only alternative for the orientation of the axis in depth is orthogonal.

Glide Drawings

Introduction

There are three families of method-oriented pictorial drawings: perspective, paraline, and glide. Each has useful applications. Perspectives effectively portray objects and environments as they appear in space viewed from eye level. Paralines communicate conceptual overviews of objects in space with great economy of means. Glides, on the other hand, depict the illusion of irregular surfaces with greater clarity than either perspectives or paralines. All three construction types have this in common: they can be easily constructed on the basis of simple rules and procedures.

This chapter describes rules and methods for quickly and painlessly constructing various useful glide-drawing variations. The methods themselves are written so that an entire glide view can be constructed without having to project from a related plan or elevation. All the methods are expedients, intended to abbreviate the drawing process by reducing the number of measured drawings and shrinking the amount of space required for their construction.

In outward appearance the glide view looks very much like a one-point perspective drawing. In fact, however, the glide view is more like a decentralized one-point perspective construction, because glides are structured around more than one vanishing pattern for related orthogonal depth parallels, whereas perspectives are not. One-point perspective parallels must always vanish towards points; glide parallels can vanish towards lines and planes as well. With glides, we are continually asking ourselves the question: ''Where does this orthogonal parallel vanish in the construction?'' This question is never asked in perspective, since all orthogonals are assumed to vanish towards a single point.

The material for this chapter is divided into three parts: in the first part, typical elements within the glide visual field are defined. In the second part, the vocabulary and definitions explained in the first part provide the basis of rules and procedures for constructing several useful glide-drawing variations. The chapter closes with a review of the general principles of glide drawings, providing examples of alternative ways to organize lateral and depth convergence effects.

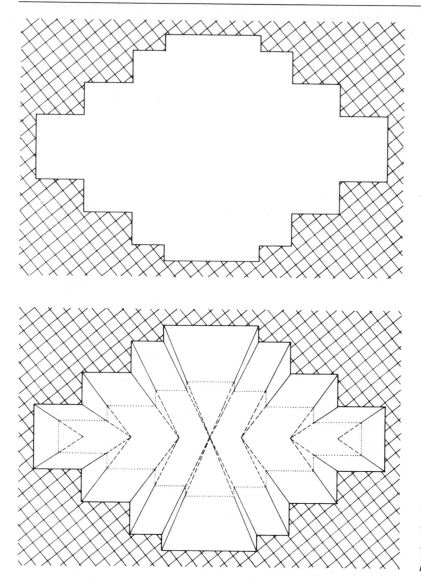

The Elements of Glide Construction

All the glide-drawing variations in this chapter are described in terms of a common vocabulary of elements and relationships. To simplify the task of defining these terms, the complete glide structure can be analyzed into these three essential parts: the names of important lines and planes within the glide visual field, the elements of glide lateral armatures, and depth-measuring devices.

Lines and Planes in the Glide Visual Field

Glide drawings are constructed with transverse and orthogonal lines and planes. Every transverse line or plane is assumed to parallel the surface of the drawing paper, existing at a constant depth within the pictorial illusion. On the other hand, every orthogonal line and plane is assumed to orient at right angles to the surface of the drawing paper, extending straight back into the pictorial illusion. There are names for several important transverse and orthogonal lines and planes.

The Picture Plane

The picture plane is an important transverse plane. It is an imaginary plane that is assumed to rest on the surface of the sheet of drawing paper. Every glide projection originates from a plan, elevation, or section that is contained in the surface of the picture plane.

The picture plane is contained in the plan, section, or elevation from which the glide is projected

The infinity plane parallels the picture plane; elements beyond the infinity plane are shown with dashed lines

The Infinity Plane

The infinity plane is another important transverse plane. It defines the limit of measured depth within the glide-drawing construction. By convention, lines and planes that exist beyond the surface of the glide transverse infinity plane are shown with dashed or broken lines.

Horizontal and Vertical Orthogonal Planes

There are two kinds of orthogonal planes in every glide construction: horizontal and vertical. However, within every horizontal or vertical orthogonal plane, there are a total of three different ways in which orthogonals can be structured to appear to recede in depth in the pictorial image. The three arrangements are called vanishing, directing, and parallel fans. A fan describes the pattern for depicting the recession of orthogonals within a horizontal or vertical plane.

The Vanishing Fan

When related parallels within an orthogonal plane appear to vanish toward a point, we shall agree to call this arrangement a vanishing fan. The vanishing fan is the planar equivalent of the three-dimensional one-point perspective vanishing-point field.

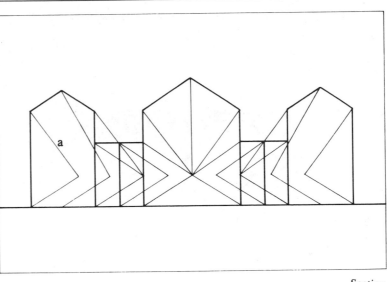

Section

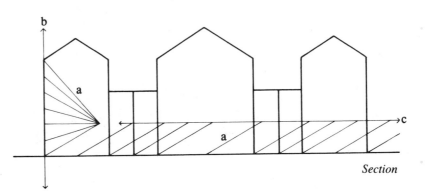

Section

a. *Orthogonal line*
b. *Vertical orthogonal plane*
c. *Horizontal orthogonal plane*

73

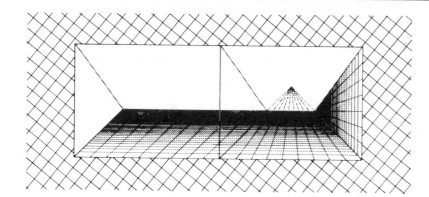

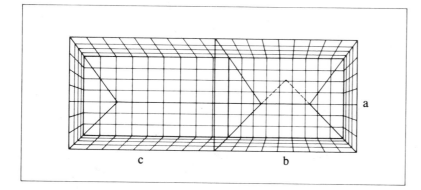

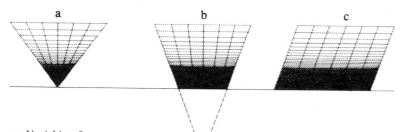

a. Vanishing fan
b. Directing fan
c. Parallel fan

The Directing Fan

When related orthogonals within a plane diminish in depth towards the limit of a vanishing line before they actually meet at a point in the distance, we shall agree to call this arrangement a directing fan. This fan separates the direction of recession of orthogonals from the measured limits of their depths within the pictorial field. Thus, a particular orthogonal line can diminish towards its vanishing point before reaching the point source that organizes its direction within the visual field. Directing fans are easy to identify because at least part of each orthogonal appears as a dashed line, indicating that portions of lines within the fan extend beyond the limits of the infinity plane. The meeting point for related orthogonals within a directing fan is called a directing point. Within a directing fan all orthogonals vanish along a vanishing axis.

The Parallel Fan

When orthogonals within a plane appear to recede in parallel towards a vanishing axis, we shall agree to call this a parallel fan. Every orthogonal within a parallel fan vanishes towards a vanishing line. The vanishing line consists of all the individual vanishing points for all the orthogonals within the plane.

The three fan arrangements, vanishing, directing, and parallel, describe the three patterned behaviors of receding orthogonals within the horizontal and vertical planes of the glide variations discussed in the next section.

The Lateral Armature

The glide lateral armature coordinates the overall patterned convergence of receding orthogonals within the glide pictorial image. It organizes the recession of orthogonals towards points, lines, and planes. The lateral armature provides an answer to the question: if related orthogonals do not vanish towards a common point, as they must in perspective constructions, then what is their order of recession? This is an important question to answer, because not all orthogonals will appear to vanish at the same point in the glide projective view.

Every lateral armature, regardless of variation, consists of three important elements: its staging rectangle, its staging orthogonals, and its staging transversals. Each of these staging elements is necessary in order to frame the pattern of recession for vanishing orthogonals within the glide view.

The Staging Rectangle and its Orthogonals

The staging rectangle is contained within the picture plane. It is constructed within the plan, elevation, or section view that is to be projected in glide. Every staging rectangle contains four staging orthogonals. These are located at the corners of the rectangle. The direction in which these orthogonals vanish within the glide view is determined by the configuration of staging transversals.

Staging Transversals

Staging transversals consist of the vanishing points, lines, and planes as well as the directing points and lines that interact with the staging orthogonals to provide the pattern for the development of all receding orthogonals within the glide view. By convention, all elements of the lateral armature that exist behind the infinity plane are shown with dashed lines. These elements include the directing axes and portions of directing fans that extend beyond their vanishing lines.

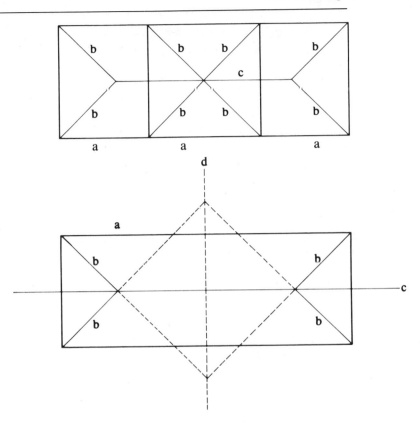

The lateral armature
a. Staging rectangle
b. Staging orthogonals
c. Vanishing axis
d. Directing axis

75

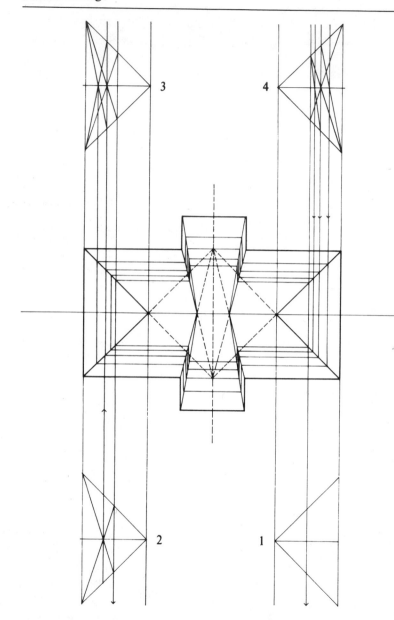

Depth-measuring Devices

Lateral armatures organize the lateral convergence pattern for all vanishing orthogonals within the glide view. The depth-measuring instrument provides the means for proportioning the depth of transverse lines and planes within the glide view. Together, these two devices, one that orders lateral convergence, the other that orders depth convergence, structure the entire glide image.

There are many ways to measure the glide depth of field. Here, we shall describe two very useful methods, both of which are based on commonsense one-point measuring-line perspective techniques.

For the sake of clarifying the structure of the depth-measuring instrument in the glide projection, we shall always draw the device off to the side of the image. With experience, this instrument can be constructed within the glide view.

The Midpoint Method

This method is based on the obvious fact that the midpoint of a rectangle in perspective can be located by constructing its diagonals. Through successive construction of diagonals within rectangles and of diagonals through the midpoints of their sides, a diminishing scale of depth measurements can be developed. These measurements can then be projected into the glide view by means of transverse lines.

The device itself consists of a simple vanishing fan that is divided into two parts by a center vanishing orthogonal line. The vanishing point for this orthogonal vanishing fan should coincide with the vanishing point for a vanishing fan within the glide construction.

The midpoint method for measuring depth

76

This assures that the measured limits of its constructed depth will not exceed the boundaries of the infinity plane.

It is customary to construct the first rectangle within the midpoint measuring frame on the basis of an initial depth judgment. This depth judgment is normally made by constructing an important transverse plane within the glide view itself, such as the primary floor plane within a glide floor plan. This transverse plane is then projected into the depth frame, and all other depth measurements are proportioned on its basis.

Just as with one-point perspective constructions, the first depth judgment should be made on the basis of what is appropriate to the given situation. Technically, it doesn't matter how deep we choose to make this first transverse plane. Realistically, the total depth of field for the glide construction should be kept as shallow as possible without sacrificing the image of the third dimension within the view. Experience is the best means for making this choice.

The Vanishing-diagonals Method

The other depth-measuring apparatus is called the vanishing-diagonals method. On first sight its structure appears less straightforward than the midpoint method. However, it achieves the same end results with this advantage: it proportions fractional depth measurements such as one-third and one-fifth.

The device itself consists of a vanishing point, a vanishing point for diagonals, a depth line, and a measuring line. The vanishing point and the vanishing point for diagonals are contained on a line that parallels the measuring line.

The vanishing-diagonals method for measuring depth

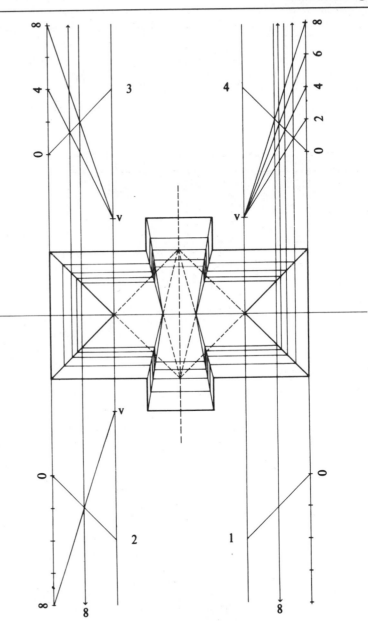

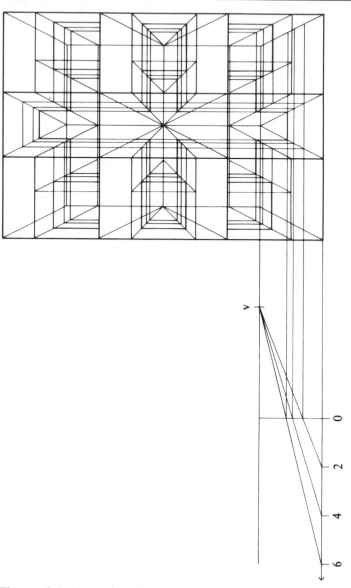

The vanishing-diagonals method for measuring depth

To proportion depths, measurements are made along the measuring line in the scale of the plan or elevation from which the glide image is constructed. These measurements project directly into depth along the depth line by means of the vanishing point for diagonals. The intersection of diagonal projectors with the depth line marks their respective projected depths. Note that measurements are scaled on either side of the depth line. Measurements scaled along the measuring line on the side away from the vanishing point for diagonals appear to project back into depth, whereas measurements scaled on the side towards the vanishing point for diagonals appear to project forward into the visual field. The measuring line and its paralleling base line, which contains the vanishing point for the depth apparatus, should be attached to a vanishing fan within the glide construction as illustrated.

The position of the vanishing point for diagonals must, of course, be known before any measured depths can be projected into the glide view. This position is normally found in three steps.
(1) A transverse plane is constructed within the glide view. Although the choice of depth for this plane is a judgment, experience suggests that it should be made as shallow as possible while retaining the pictorial qualities of the depicted surface.
(2) The depth of this transverse plane is projected by means of transverse lines into the depth frame.
(3) The actual depth of the constructed transverse plane, as measured from the surface of the picture plane, is marked off on the measuring line.

The position of the vanishing point for diagonals is found by constructing a line through the actual and projected depth measurements, which lie along the measuring line and the depth line, respectively, and by marking its intersection with the base line. Once the vanishing point for diagonals has been located, all other depths can be measured and projected.

How to Construct Glide Drawings

Glide drawings may take many different forms. In the previous chapter, we described six individual glide-drawing variations, called the herringbone, the vanishing point, the vanishing axis, the vanishing plane, the keystone, and the box. There are also a number of core and series component glide constructions, each consisting of more than one armature within the same glide view. In addition, there are scaled and freeform glide variations.

It would not be possible to describe every single glide variation here. That would be like attempting to document separate rules and procedures for constructing every conceivable paraline-drawing variation, of which there are many. Instead, we shall focus our attention on methods for constructing several of the most useful glide-drawing variations.

Before proceeding with our discussion of glide methods, the reader should keep in mind that many of the terms used here to describe glide drawings were originally defined in the first part of this chapter. If a particular word or phrase should happen to look unfamiliar, return to the first section in order to find its meaning.

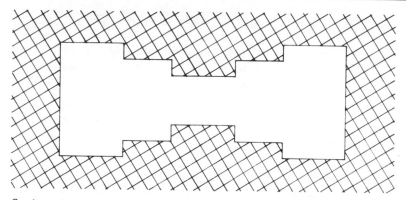

Section

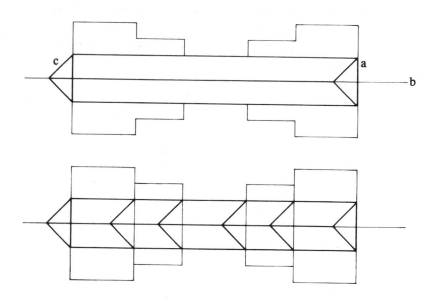

How to Construct the Herringbone Glide Drawing

The herringbone glide configuration is useful for depicting very long and narrow, yet shallow pictorial views. Because its structure can be extended laterally to any length, the herringbone is well adapted to the pictorial representation of street facades, for example, or aerial views of long and narrow city corridors. Here is the procedure for constructing a herringbone glide view of a long and narrow surface.

The Setup

Begin with the plan, elevation or section view of a long and narrow, yet shallow surface, drawn to any convenient scale. The glide drawing will be projected within this view.

The Lateral-armature Construction

(1) Construct the staging rectangle for the lateral armature within the given view. Although this rectangle can be located inside, outside, or in between the boundaries of the given space, it is a good idea to construct it along principal lines of the given plan or elevation view. That way, the orientation and vanishing points for many orthogonals will be easier to find.

(2) Construct the lateral armature's vanishing axis. This axis, which parallels the long sides of the staging rectangle, can be located anywhere within the boundaries of the rectangle. It does not have to be located along the centerline of the staging rectangle.

a. Staging rectangle
b. Vanishing axis
c. Staging orthogonals

80

(3) Construct four staging orthogonals at the corners of the staging rectangle. These orthogonals should vanish towards two points on the vanishing axis. The angle that these orthogonals make with the vanishing axis is unimportant, as long as orthogonals on the same side of the vanishing axis remain parallel to each other.

Observe that the staging orthogonals define the edges in depth of four orthogonal fans. These fans are the walls that define the wedge-like space that recedes from the staging rectangle and vanishes towards the vanishing axis. Two of these fans are vertical vanishing fans; the other two are horizontal parallel fans. These fans provide the pattern template for developing all other fans in the herringbone visual field, which consists of nothing but vertical vanishing fans and horizontal parallel fans.

Orthogonals within the Lateral Armature

The lateral armature provides the referent framework for constructing vanishing orthogonal lines within the glide view. It gives us the visual clues that we need in order to know which way to orient receding orthogonals. In the case of the herringbone glide construction, every orthogonal vanishes towards the vanishing axis. To find the vanishing point for an orthogonal line that does not project from the staging rectangle itself, we need only find the vanishing point for the vertical fan that contains its plan, elevation or section image point.

On the basis of the staging pattern alone, you should be able to locate the vanishing point for every orthogonal within the glide view. However, for the benefit of those who may have trouble visualizing the overall pattern, it is possible, although involved, to describe a procedure.

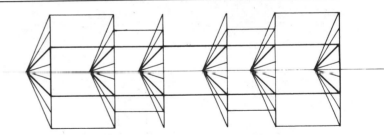

Vertical orthogonal vanishing fans

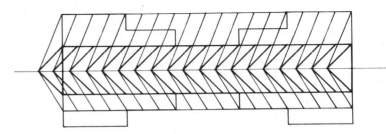

Horizontal orthogonal parallel fans

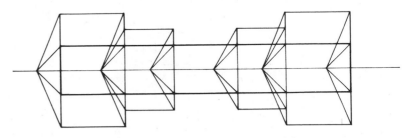

Combined horizontal and vertical orthogonal fans

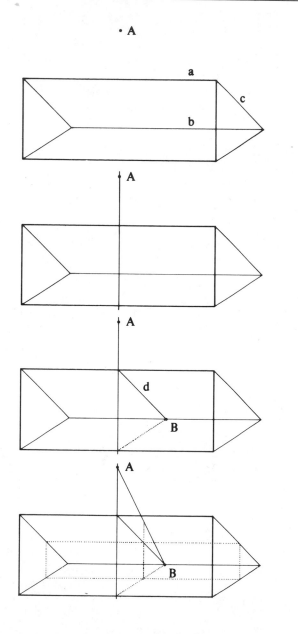

To find the vanishing point for an orthogonal line, labeled A, that is located in the plan view somewhere above the staging rectangle, construct a light vertical trace through its image point in the plan or elevation view; note the trace's intersection with the staging rectangle; find the vanishing point for the orthogonal that begins where the vertical trace intersects the staging rectangle. We will call this orthogonal B. Because vanishing orthogonal B is contained within a parallel staging fan, its parallel vanishing direction can be constructed, and consequently its vanishing point along the vanishing axis located. However, this is also the vanishing point for the orthogonal A, because both orthogonals are contained in the same vertical vanishing fan.

This process can be repeated over and over again in order to find the location of the vanishing point along the vanishing axis for every orthogonal line within the visual field. Once this procedure is understood, the remaining construction problem is to measure the depths of all transverse planes.

Depth Measurements

To measure depth in herringbone glide drawings, simply attach a vanishing-diagonal or midpoint depth-measuring instrument to one of the construction's vertical vanishing fans. Both these instruments, along with the procedure for measuring depths, are described in greater detail in the first part of this chapter.

In essence, the procedure involves making an initial depth judgment and then structuring all depths in proportion to this judgment. Remember to keep the depth of field shallow but not too shallow. The

Locating the vanishing point for an orthogonal line (A)

deeper the projection, the greater the distortion; yet, if the projection is too shallow, there will be no sense of depth in the drawing. Observe that in linking the measuring device to a vanishing fan, no transverse plane extends beyond the depth of the vanishing axis.

Coordinate Lines and Planes

Points within the glide image can be found only by projecting along orthogonal lines and within transverse planes. No other vanishing lines or directions can be used to find the images of points within the drawing. Thus, angled lines and planes and irregular curves should be constructed in the glide view either by finding their endpoints and connecting them or by breaking their lengths into smaller segments, plotting their points, and connecting these. This is not an unusual way in which to construct pictorial drawings. In fact, it is similar to the process that is used for constructing paraline drawings.

Noncoordinate Lines and Planes

There are a few eccentric pictorial effects that may occur within a herringbone construction. These are distortion problems that are more likely to be noticed if the glide view is made too deep. Here, we shall briefly review their characteristics.

Noncoordinate lines and planes in depth will behave in different ways, depending upon the type of vanishing plane that contains them. For example, an oblique or angled line that is constructed within an orthogonal vanishing fan will appear as a straight line in the glide construction. This is normal.

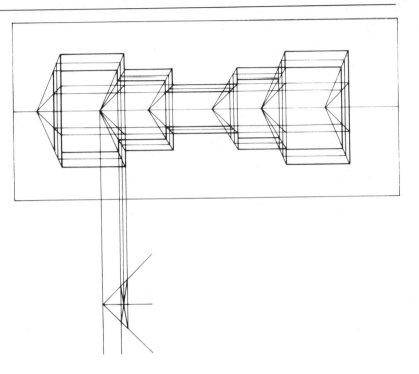

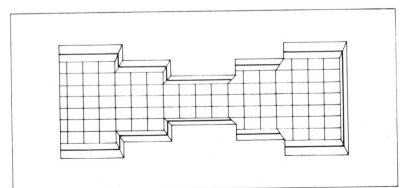

A midpoint depth-measuring device attached to the herringbone lateral armature

83

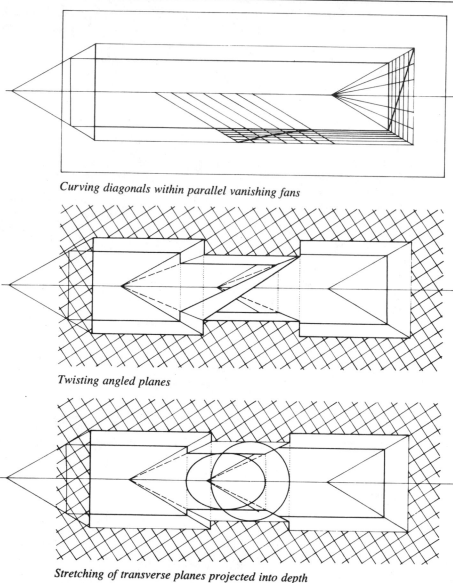

Curving diagonals within parallel vanishing fans

Twisting angled planes

Stretching of transverse planes projected into depth

But an oblique or angled line that is constructed within a parallel or directing fan will appear to curve. The extent of this curvature is dependent upon the depth of the glide view. If the view is very shallow, the curvature of an oblique line within a directing or parallel fan will be subtle. In fact, its curvature will hardly be noticed, and, for practical purposes, the line can be drawn with straightedge alone.

Transverse noncoordinate lines will appear as straight lines within the glide view, regardless of the depth of the transverse plane that contains them. However, an angled transverse line will appear to twist as it is projected in depth. That is, the original angle of orientation for the noncoordinate line, which is its orientation in the picture plane, will rotate as the line is projected into depth.

Another interesting pictorial effect occurs whenever shapes within the original plan or elevation view are projected to deeper transverse planes. For example, a circle in plan projects to a transverse plane in depth as an ellipse; a square in elevation projects as a rectangle. As with other eccentric glide pictorial effects, problems with shape distortion can be minimized by keeping the glide projection shallow.

Eccentric pictorial effects

84

The Keystone, the Vanishing Point, the Vanishing Plane, and the Box

The herringbone and the vanishing-axis glide, which are discussed separately, are by far the two most useful glide-drawing configurations. Four other glide variations, although easily constructed, are nonetheless limited in application. These include the keystone, the box, the vanishing-point, and the vanishing-plane glide drawing. We shall only briefly mention the structure of these four glide variations here.

The Keystone Glide Construction

Keystone and herringbone glides have similar structures. Both use the same lateral convergence pattern. Hence, the method for finding the direction of recession for a vanishing orthogonal is the same in both constructions. The difference between the two is in the location of their infinity planes. Orthogonals within the herringbone visual field appear to vanish towards an axis; keystone orthogonals vanish towards a plane.

To construct the keystone vanishing plane configuration, bring its infinity plane, which is defined by a depth-measuring device, closer to the viewer by attaching the measuring device to an orthogonal fan so that the vanishing point for the depth apparatus is shallower than the orthogonal fan's lateral convergence point.

When an orthogonal fan is structured in this way, it is called a directing fan. The concept of the directing fan is explained in detail in the first part of this chapter. Because every orthogonal line within the keystone construction diminishes to infinity before it reaches its directing point, there is no vanishing axis. What would be the

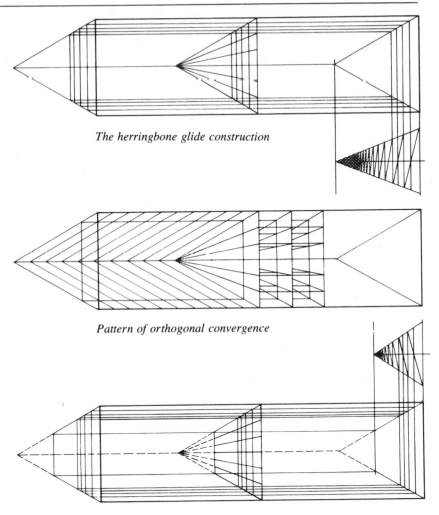

The herringbone glide construction

Pattern of orthogonal convergence

The keystone glide construction with shallower infinity plane

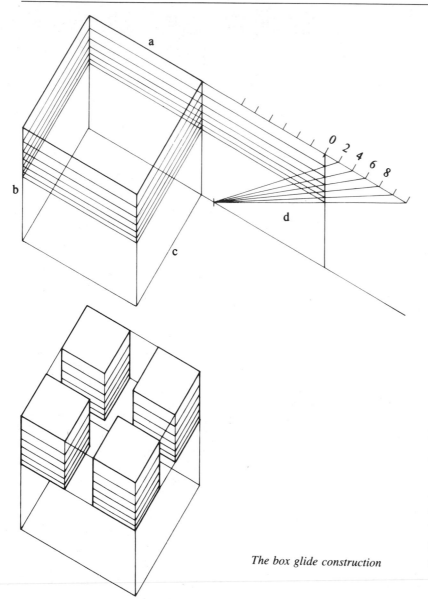

The box glide construction

vanishing axis within a herringbone construction is located on the other side of the keystone infinity plane, not within it. It is therefore called a directing axis and indicated with a dashed line. In essence, the keystone glide can be thought of as a compressed herringbone glide.

The lateral armature that organizes the recession of orthogonals within the glide view is the same in both herringbone and keystone constructions. So is the rule that permits projecting only along orthogonals and within transverse planes. What varies is the way in which the depth-measuring apparatus is attached to an orthogonal fan. In the herringbone construction, the orthogonal fan becomes a vanishing fan. In the keystone, it becomes a directing fan.

The Box Glide Construction

The box glide looks like an ordinary paraline drawing. In fact, box glides and paralines differ only in that the box glide has an infinity plane. There is diminution of scale along the receding orthogonals within a box glide drawing. The boundaries for this infinity plane are defined with a depth-measuring device of the sort mentioned earlier in this chapter. Box glides can be thought of as compressed paralines.

The Vanishing-point and Vanishing-area Glide Constructions

Like box glides, vanishing-point and vanishing-plane constructions are really intended to be used as parts of component glide drawings, which are described later in this chapter. However, both vanishing-point and vanishing-area constructions can be discussed as independent drawing forms.

The vanishing-point glide is similar in outward appearance to the one-point perspective. In fact, it differs only in the shape of the projective visual field. The glide visual field is shaped like a tunnel and diminishes to a point in the distance, whereas the perspective visual field is shaped like a pyramid and is assumed to expand in the distance of the pictorial space.

Just as the keystone glide can be interpreted as a compressed version of the herringbone configuration, so the vanishing-area glide can be interpreted as a compressed one-point glide drawing. Again, spatial compression is achieved by introducing a depth-measuring device whose vanishing point describes the limits of an infinity plane that is located closer to the viewer than the construction's center projective point.

Thus, for every receding orthogonal within a vanishing-plane construction, convergence in depth occurs before the line itself meets with other orthogonals at the center convergence point of the construction. Lateral and depth convergence are separate. By convention, elements located on the other side of the infinity plane are indicated with dashed lines. In particular, the glide one-point center vanishing point is the directing center point within vanishing-area constructions.

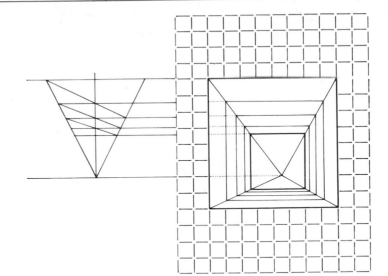

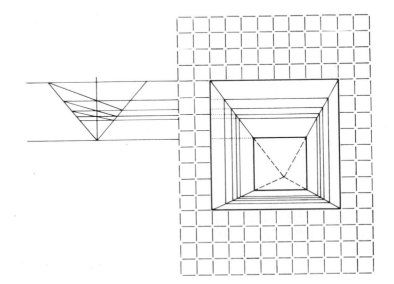

(above) Vanishing-point glide
(below) Vanishing-area glide with shallower infinity plane

87

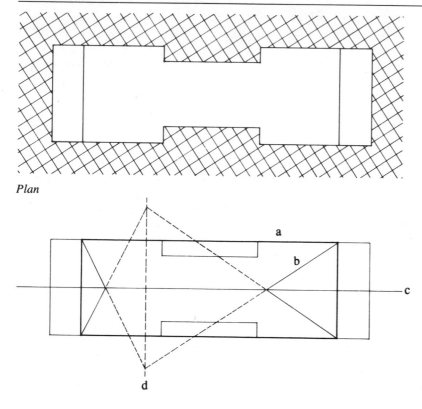

Plan

a. *Staging rectangle*
b. *Staging orthogonal*
c. *Vanishing axis*
d. *Directing axis*

How to Construct Vanishing-axis Glide Drawings

In outward appearance, Zanini's method for constructing traveling vanishing-point illusions closely resembles the vanishing-axis construction. The resemblance between the two is only superficial, however, because each has a different underlying structure. Zanini's construction was merely an effect without projective underpinnings. Vanishing-axis constructions, based on the principles of glide projection, integrate horizontal and vertical vanishing fans more completely than Zanini's construction. For that matter, vanishing-axis glides are the most unified and visually integrated glide projective form. Unfortunately, because the vanishing fans within vanishing-axis constructions are interwoven, they are slightly more difficult to understand. The procedure for constructing a typical vanishing-axis glide drawing consists of the following.

The Setup

Begin with the plan, elevation, or section view of a shallow rectangular space, drawn to an appropriate scale.

The Lateral Armature

The vanishing-axis lateral armature organizes the lateral convergence of orthogonals within the visual field. To construct this armature, follow these simple steps.

(1) Place a staging rectangle over the plan, elevation, or section view that is to be projected.

(2) Construct a vanishing axis and a directing axis. These axes should be arranged so that the vanishing axis runs in the longer

direction of the staging rectangle. The axes should parallel the edges of the staging rectangle, but they do not have to pass through the midpoint of the staging rectangle. The vanishing and directing axes can be located anywhere within the boundaries of the staging rectangle.

(3) Construct four staging orthogonals. These orthogonals must cross the vanishing axis at only two points and must meet on the directing axis at only two points. The angle that these staging orthogonals make with the vanishing axis does not affect the accuracy of the construction of the drawing. Note that all lines on the other side of the infinity plane, which include all lines beyond the depth of the vanishing axis, are indicated as dashed lines.

The Behavior of Orthogonals Within Vertical and Horizontal Fans

The lateral armature defines the pattern of recession for all receding orthogonals within the glide view. To find the location of the vanishing point on the vanishing axis for orthogonal lines within the glide visual field, it is necessary to understand the behavior of vertical and horizontal orthographic fans.

Observe that all vertical fans are vanishing fans — that is, every orthogonal within a vertical orthogonal plane vanishes to a common point on the vanishing axis. On the other hand, every horizontal orthogonal fan is a directing fan. Thus, every orthogonal line within a particular horizontal orthogonal plane converges towards a common directing point on the directing axis, yet each orthogonal vanishes in depth towards a point along the vanishing axis.

Rather than untangle a complicated step-by-step procedure for lo-

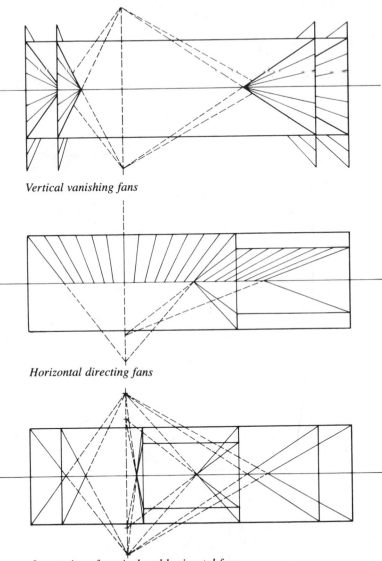

Vertical vanishing fans

Horizontal directing fans

Interaction of vertical and horizontal fans

89

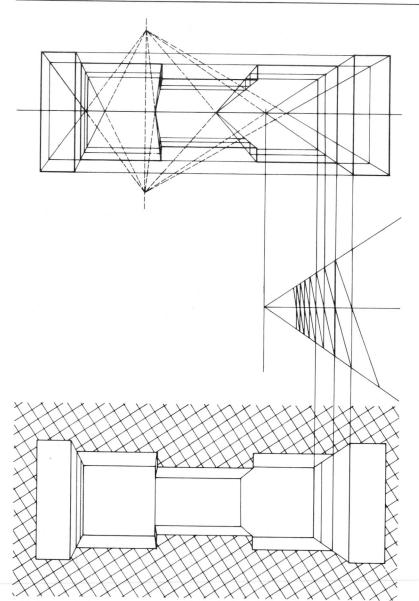

cating the vanishing point for a particular orthogonal here, just keep in mind that all orthogonals vanish along a single common vanishing axis. With the help of the illustration and with a little practice at sketching the pattern of recession for various orthogonals, you should be able to locate the vanishing point for any orthogonal within the glide visual field with ease.

Making Depth Measurements

The procedure for finding depths within the vanishing-axis construction is the same as it is for all other glide-drawing variations. Begin by attaching a depth-measuring device, either a midpoint or vanishing-diagonals instrument, to the construction, aligning the device's vanishing point with the vanishing point for a vertical vanishing fan. Then, make an initial depth judgment within the glide view itself and project this depth into the measuring device. Scale all other depths within the device on the basis of this judgment. All depths project around the glide construction along transverse lines and within transverse planes.

Of course, as is true of all glide variations, the vanishing-axis view will be less distorted if it is kept reasonably shallow. For a complete explanation regarding the process for making initial depth judgments and for measuring all depths within the glide view, consult the first part of this chapter.

A depth-measuring device attached to the vanishing-axis construction

Noncoordinate Lines and Planes

All measured constructions should occur within horizontal and vertical orthogonal planes. All depths must be projected along orthogonals. Nonorthogonal and nontransverse lines and planes should be constructed by first plotting and then connecting endpoints.

Eccentric Pictorial Effects

Certain unusual pictorial effects are liable to occur within the glide vanishing-axis construction, particularly if the depth of view is made too deep. Angled lines that are constructed on the surface of orthogonal directing fans will appear to curve. This curvature is subtle if angled lines are constructed within shallow projective fields.

On the other hand, nonaxial transverse lines will remain straight upon projection, but will change their orientation when projected. This twisting effect is similar to the effect that was described for herringbone constructions.

Finally, shapes in the original plan or elevation view will undergo a sort of stretching action as they are projected into depth. Transverse squares will project as rectangles, and circles will project as ellipses. The extent of this stretching action is related to the depth of the projection. The shallower the projection, the less the distortion. For very shallow glide views, the change in shape is barely noticeable.

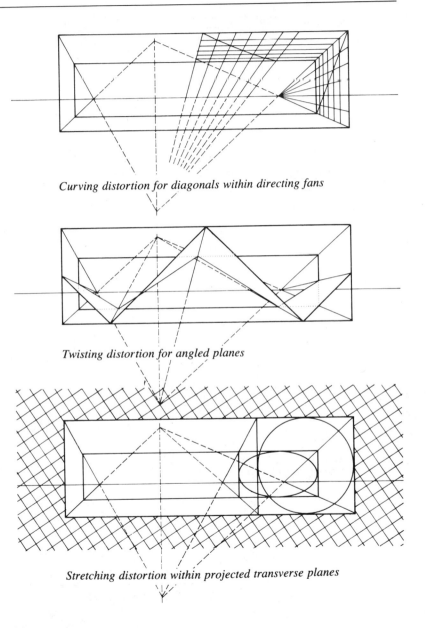

Curving distortion for diagonals within directing fans

Twisting distortion for angled planes

Stretching distortion within projected transverse planes

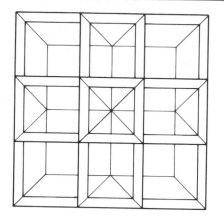

Core component glide

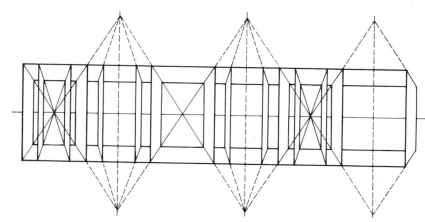

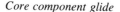

Repeating-series component glide

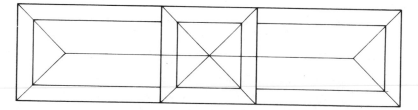

Nonrepeating-series component glide

Component Glide Drawings

So far, we have studied methods and procedures for structuring individual glide-drawing variations. Characteristic of each variation is the sweeping continuity of the single lateral armature that defines the lateral convergence pattern for the entire pictorial image. Pictorial illusions are almost always structured in this way. For example, continuous depth and lateral convergence patterns are taken for granted in paraline and perspective constructions.

Yet, it is structurally feasible to combine different drawing variations within the same pictorial image. For instance, paraline and perspective, or axonometric and isometric, can be combined to create coherent visual fields that may or may not be of practical benefit in communicating three-dimensional form.

Multiple lateral armatures may also be combined to create useful glide images. The glide visual field can be partitioned to accommodate multiple lateral and depth convergence patterns. When more than one lateral armature occurs within the same pictorial image, it is called a component glide drawing.

Core and Series Constructions

There are many ways to pattern the arrangement of multiple armatures within a single glide view. In general, these arrangements fall into two categories: core and series constructions. Core component configurations consist of multiple lateral armatures that are arranged to emphasize the center of the glide projection; series configurations, which often make use of diverging lateral armatures, are patterned into linear repeating or nonrepeating sequences of lateral glide armatures.

The Two Rules of Assembly

Regardless of whether the component construction is core or series, by definition its structure must join together with no gaps or overlaps between armatures and consist of an infinity plane that is common to all its lateral armatures. Within the limits of these rules, there are opportunities for putting together many different combinations of lateral armatures.

We cannot discuss every core and series component glide variation here. There are too many combinations. Instead, we shall briefly describe the procedure for constructing two of the most useful core component variations. The inquisitive reader should be able to put together other component glides on the basis of the patterns of these two cases.

The Core Component Construction

Every core component glide drawing consists of two or more of the six core lateral armatures, shown at right. In essence, the lateral armatures within a core component glide drawing join together so that the edges and planes that define the subject matter of the construction vanish in accordance to the pattern of their respective bounding staging rectangles.

1. *Vanishing point*
2. *Vanishing plane*
3. *Vanishing axis*
4. *Herringbone*
5. *Keystone*
6. *Box*

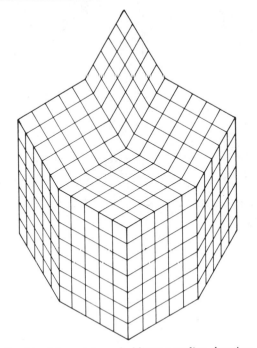

Combined isometric and oblique paraline drawing

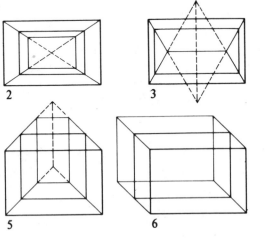

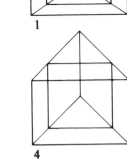

93

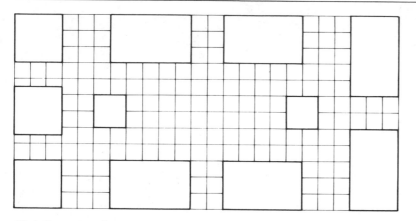

Plan view

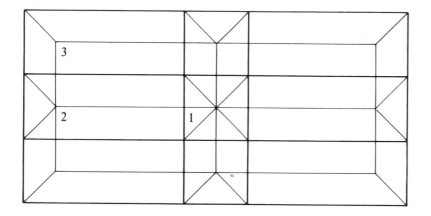

Staging rectangle
1. *Vanishing-point armature*
2. *Herringbone armature*
3. *Box armature*

Core Component Variations

The double herringbone and the eggcrate configurations are two of the most basic and useful core component constructions. The double-herringbone glide drawing consists of a vanishing-point lateral armature between two herringbone armatures. The eggcrate glide consists of a center vanishing-point armature located at the juncture of four herringbone constructions, with box lateral armatures at its corners.

The eggcrate glide structure could be compressed by moving the infinity plane closer to the picture plane. This structure would then consist of a vanishing-plane armature, four keystone armatures, and four box armatures. In a similar manner, we could compress the double herringbone arrangement by moving the infinity plane closer to the surface of the glide drawing. This structure would then consist of a vanishing-area armature flanked by two keystone armatures. Many other component glide arrangements are possible.

How to Construct an Eggcrate Glide Drawing

An eggcrate glide drawing can be projected from the plan, section, or elevation view of any shallow surface configuration. The procedure for projecting its three-dimensional image is the same as that suggested for constructing individual glide variations.

(1) Construct the staging rectangle by dividing the plan, section, or elevation into nine rectangular areas. It is best to coordinate the edges of the staging rectangle with important horizontal and vertical elements within the floor plan. In this regard, it is not necessary to make the individual staging rectangles symmetrical. They can be proportioned to fit the principal lines of the scheme.

(2) Construct horizontal and vertical vanishing axes. Their intersec-

tion can occur anywhere within the boundaries of the center staging rectangle. These vanishing axes are contained within the infinity plane.

(3) Construct the staging orthogonals for each of the nine lateral armatures. Note that adjacent armatures share common orthogonals. This prevents the projection from developing undefined spaces between armatures.

Each of the eggcrate's lateral armatures defines the pattern of recession for all orthogonals within its boundaries. Every orthogonal that is contained within the boundaries of a particular lateral armature must vanish in accordance with the pattern of that armature. We can know which orthogonal belongs to which lateral armature by observing the position of the orthogonal in the plan or elevation view.

In the example, note that every orthogonal within the one-point structure vanishes towards its center vanishing point, which is located at the intersection of the two vanishing axes. Every orthogonal contained within each of the four herringbone armatures vanishes towards an axis. Finally, all the orthogonals within the box armatures appear to remain parallel to each other as they vanish towards the infinity plane. Observe that the infinity plane is contained within the same transverse plane as the vanishing axes.

The procedure for proportioning depth is just like the one that is used for all individual glide-drawing variations. First, connect a midpoint or a vanishing-diagonal depth-measuring device to a vanishing fan within the lateral armature. Be sure to coordinate the relative depths of their vanishing points. Both of these devices are described in the

Vanishing diagonals depth-measuring device attached to eggcrate armature

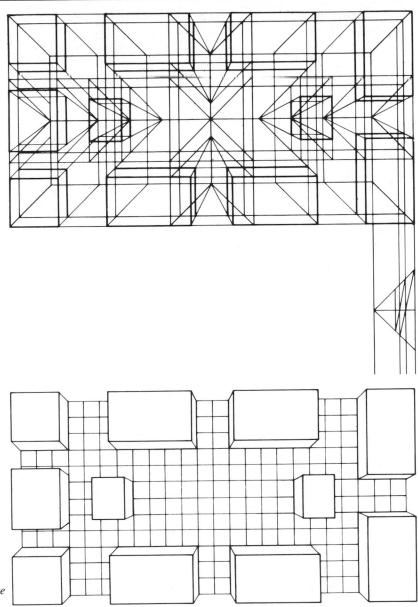

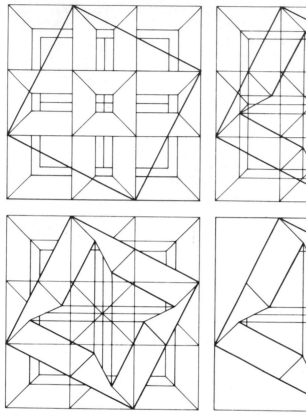

Plan view

first part of this chapter. Then, construct a transverse plane within the glide image. Make a judgment as to a reasonable depth for this plane. Project this known depth into the depth-measuring device. Use this depth to proportion other depths within the glide image. If you need more information regarding the process for projecting depths, see the first part of this chapter, where depth-measuring instruments are described in greater detail.

Do all construction along the three coordinate axes of the glide construction. Noncoordinate lines and planes should be constructed by connecting their endpoints.

All the eccentric pictorial effects that occur within individual lateral armatures may also occur within the eggcrate component construction. For information about a particular eccentric pictorial effect, consult the procedure for the individual armature in question.

There is one eccentric pictorial effect that can occur only within component glide constructions. The projected images of nonaxial transverse lines will appear to bend as they cross from one lateral armature into another. It is therefore wise to keep nonaxial lines within the boundaries of staging rectangles or, if this is not possible, to limit the depth of the projected view.

Nonaxial orthogonal planes appear to bend between armatures

How to Construct a Double-Herringbone Glide Drawing

The double-herringbone glide drawing consists of the three adjacent lateral armatures that make up the middle axis of an eggcrate glide. Thus, the procedure for constructing double-herringbone images is similar to that for constructing eggcrate glides.

If we begin with, say, the plan view of a long and narrow site, we can divide the plan into three rectangles. These rectangles are the staging rectangles for the double-herringbone configuration. They can be sized to fit over important shapes within the plan view. Through the staging rectangles, construct a vanishing axis, which need not be positioned symmetrically within the rectangles.

Locate a vanishing point on the vanishing axis within the boundaries of the center staging rectangle. This vanishing point defines the convergence point for all orthogonals within the limits of this middle rectangle.

Four staging orthogonals vanish towards the center point of the middle armature. These staging orthogonals must be paralleled by the corner staging orthogonals for the top and bottom herringbone staging rectangles. The framework for lateral armatures is complete.

All orthogonals within the glide view must vanish in accordance with the lateral armature in which they are contained. Further, the construction of all lines and planes within the glide visual field must then be carried out along the three coordinate axes of the projection.

The depths of all transverse lines and planes can be proportioned with a depth-measuring device of the sort described for eggcrate glides. The eccentric effects that apply to double-herringbone constructions are described under eggcrate constructions.

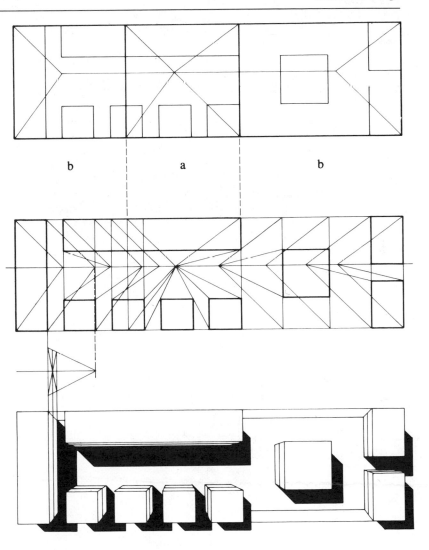

Double-herringbone construction
a. Vanishing-point armature
b. Herringbone armature

97

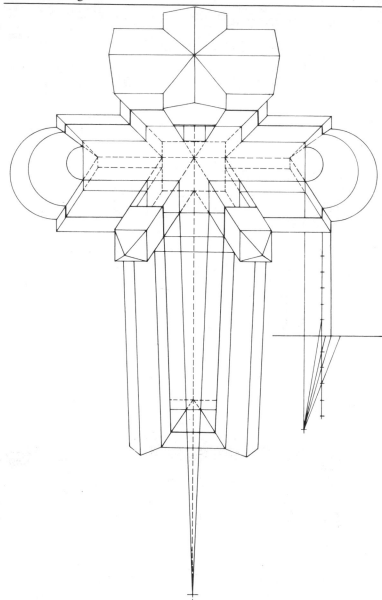

Alternative Glide Drawing Configurations

Glide drawings are not limited to the variations discussed on the previous pages. There are many other possible structures. We shall end this chapter with a summary of general glide principles along with suggestions for alternative configurations.

The system of glide drawings is closed under the following two conditions: there should be no gaps or overlaps within or between lateral armatures, and the entire pictorial image should have a common infinity plane. The gaps-and-overlaps rule governs the behavior of receding orthogonal lines and planes within the glide view. The infinity plane controls the depth of transverse lines and planes.

Freeform Glide Drawings

Freeform glide drawings consist of all the glide armature configurations that are not core or component yet are consistent within the limits of the orthogonal gaps-and-overlaps rule stated above. Diverging and converging lateral armatures can be combined in any number or order; transverse lines and planes might be radiused or curved; and the whole projective field may be partial rather than whole.

The complexity of unraveling the interconnections between various freeform alternatives is beyond the scope of this book. Two of the many possible alternative convergence patterns are illustrated here. One construction makes use of a lateral armature that is a cross between a herringbone and a keystone. The other example illustrates multiple connected armatures.

This freeform glide makes use of a hybrid lateral armature

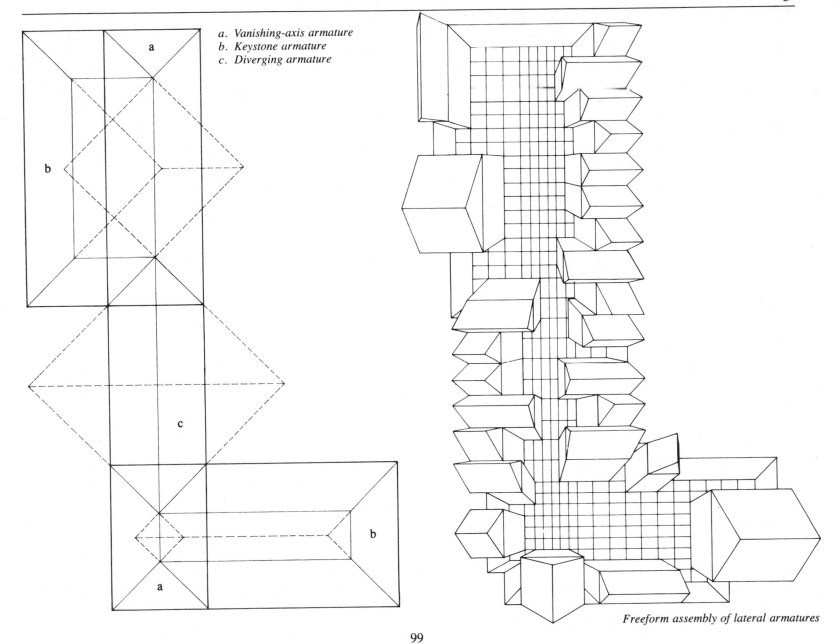

a. *Vanishing-axis armature*
b. *Keystone armature*
c. *Diverging armature*

a

b

c

a

b

Freeform assembly of lateral armatures

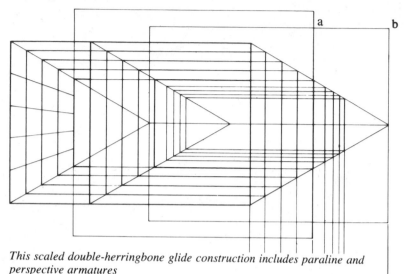

This scaled double-herringbone glide construction includes paraline and perspective armatures

Diminishing and scaled depth intervals may combine within the same glide view

a. *Transverse plane dividing scaled and diminishing intervals*
b. *Infinity plane*
c. *Scaled depth intervals*
d. *Diminishing depth intervals*

To fully appreciate freeform drawings, keep in mind that they are not intended be viewed all at once from a single position in front of the image, as in perspective, but rather they should be observed one part at a time, in a continuous sweeping or gliding motion, as in the process of viewing the earth's landscape from the cockpit of an airplane. There is local believability everywhere within a freeform glide, but no single position from which to take in the overall unity of the whole.

Scaled Glide Drawings

There are many ways to organize the recession for related orthogonals within glide drawings. In fact, glide-drawing variations are named after their orthogonal convergence patterns. Yet, all of these variations are based on only one depth-measuring system. The diminution of transversals, governed by the depth-measuring device and limited by the infinity plane, has remained constant from one glide variation to another.

Is the depth-measuring device the only conceivable way to order the glide depth of field? The answer is no. In fact, there are other ways to measure depth, one of which is very practical. Depth measurements can be scaled directly along the length of an orthogonal field line, provided they do not reach the infinity plane.

In theory, to preserve the integrity of the infinity plane, scaled measurements must not be allowed to exceed the depth of a transverse plane located at some arbitrary distance in front of the infinity plane. Measurements on the other side of this transverse plane must be calibrated with the diminishing intervals of a depth-measuring device. The reason for this restriction is obvious: every glide orthogonal plane consists of either parallel or convergent orthogonal lines. If all the receding orthogonals within the glide construction are parallel, depths can be measured to scale and there is no need for an infinity plane. However, this is actually the definition of a para-line or composite paraline drawing, not a glide.

On the other hand, if at least one plane within the glide drawing consists of convergent orthogonals, then there must be an infinity plane, which is a transverse plane that exists no deeper than the point of intersection of convergent orthogonals. Unfortunately, with an infinity plane, scaled measurements may easily exceed the limits of orthogonal convergence at infinity. To prevent this from happening, an imaginary transverse plane within the glide construction can be used to define the boundary between scaled and diminishing depth intervals. The limits of measured infinity will therefore be preserved.

Every glide-drawing variation can be scaled. The procedure is straightforward. Instead of attaching a depth-measuring device to the glide armature, a transverse plane can be constructed to define the boundary between scaled and diminishing depth intervals. Depths can then be scaled directly with a ruler along a preselected orthogonal line. If a line or plane should happen to exceed the depth of the bounding transverse plane, a depth-measuring device can be introduced to position its depth along the orthogonal measuring line.

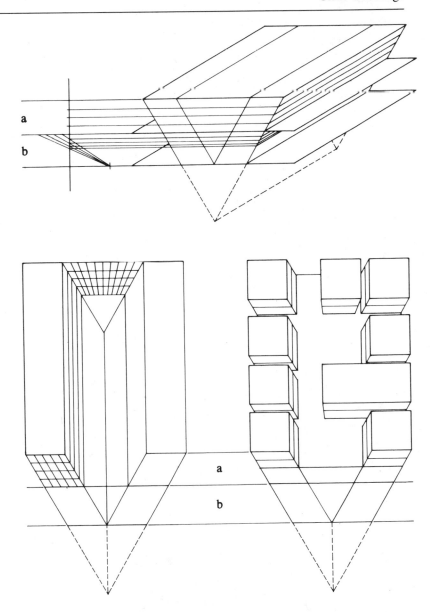

a. Scaled depth intervals
b. Diminishing depth intervals

Glide Applications

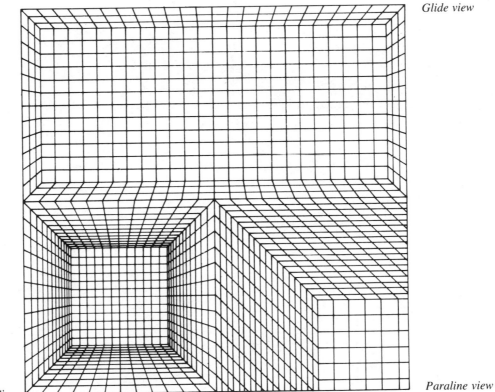

Glide view

Perspective view

Paraline view

Glide drawings are useful for depicting the plan, site plan, section, or trompe l'oeil views of buildings, interiors, or landscapes in low spatial relief. To illustrate the many uses for glide drawings, this chapter not only presents selected examples but also compares completed glide constructions with other pictorial drawing forms. What does the same aerial view of a building or landscape look like when it is illustrated in both glide and perspective? In this chapter, the reader is invited to compare the visual results.

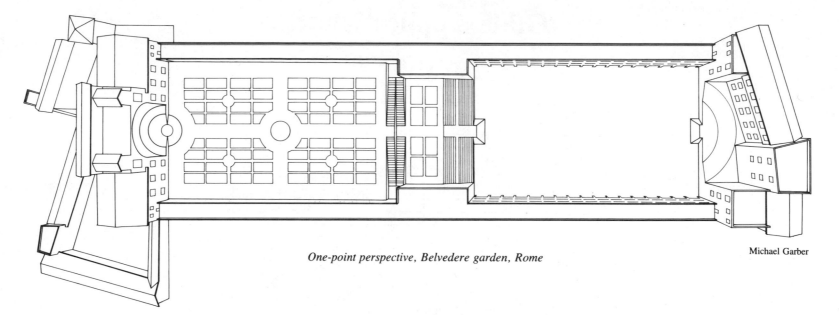

One-point perspective, Belvedere garden, Rome

Michael Garber

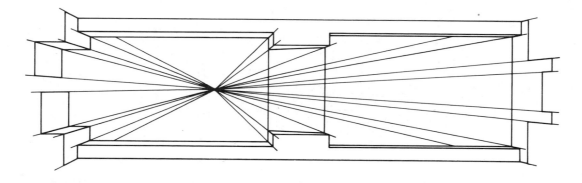

One-point armature

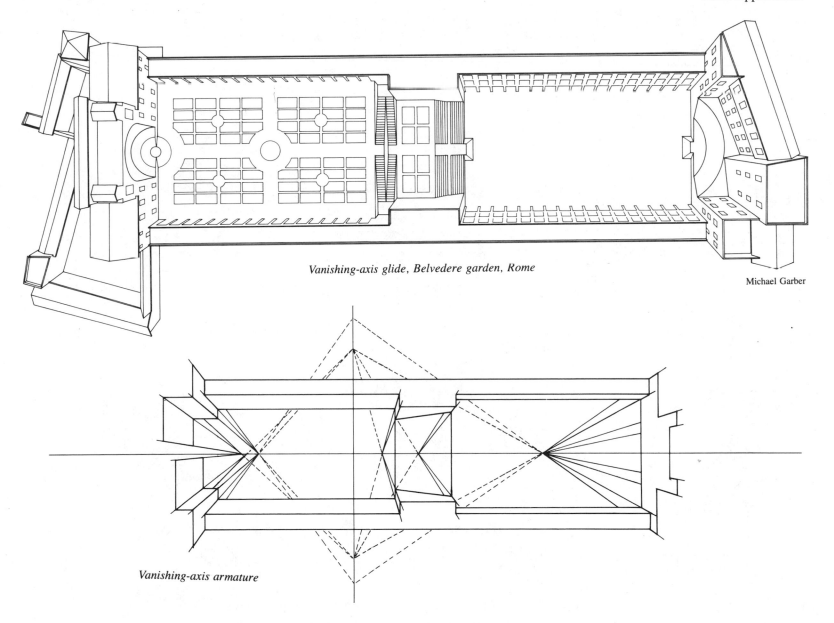

Vanishing-axis glide, Belvedere garden, Rome

Michael Garber

Vanishing-axis armature

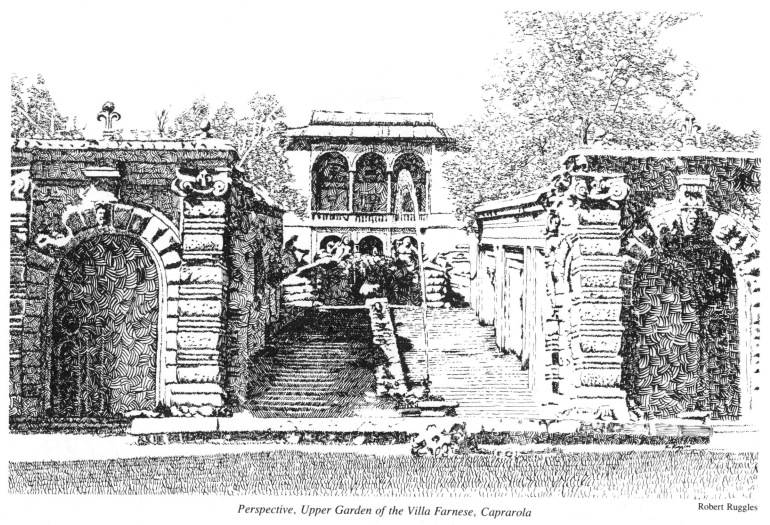

Perspective, Upper Garden of the Villa Farnese, Caprarola

Robert Ruggles

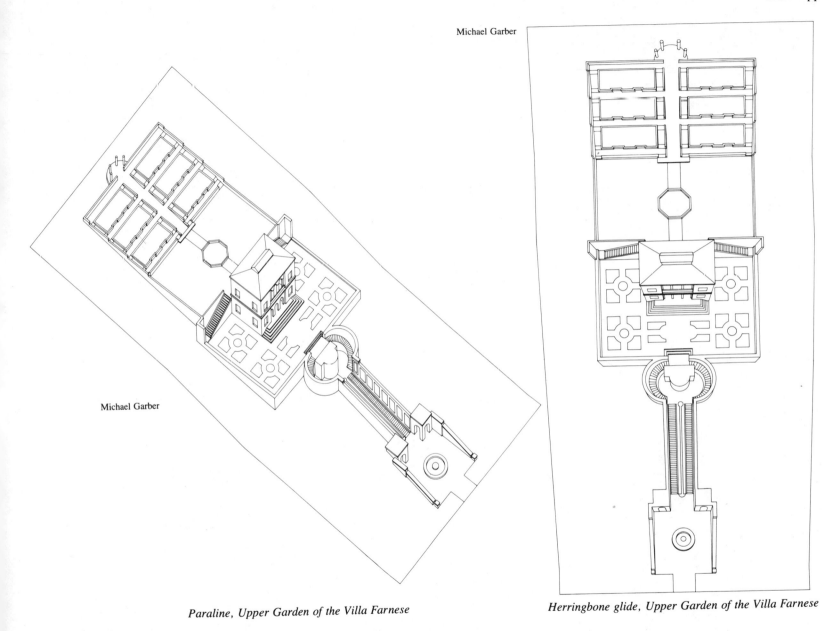

Michael Garber

Michael Garber

Paraline, Upper Garden of the Villa Farnese

Herringbone glide, Upper Garden of the Villa Farnese

107

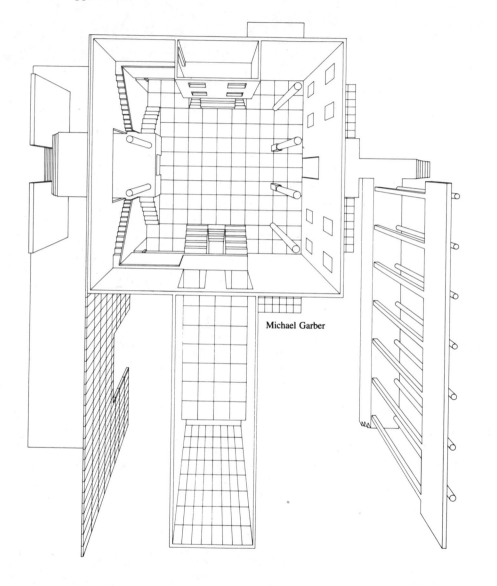

Michael Garber

Aerial-perspective one-point view into courtyard

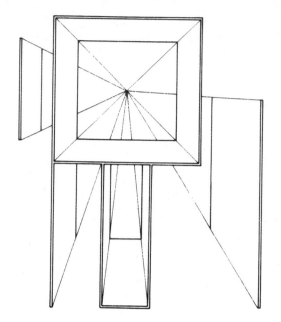

One-point armature

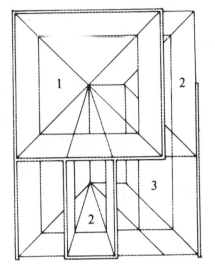

Component armature
1. *One-point*
2. *Herringbone*
3. *Box*

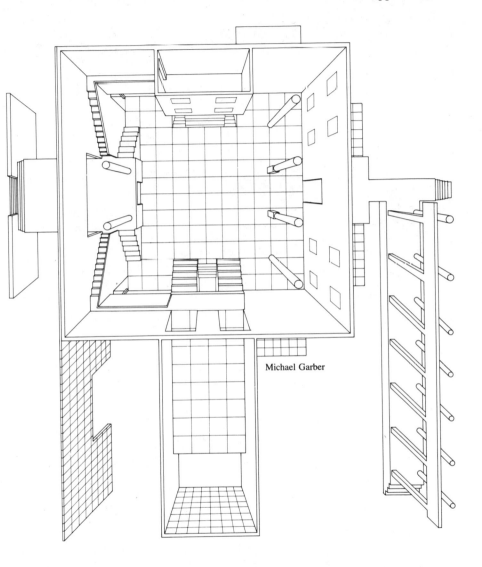

Michael Garber

Core component glide view into courtyard

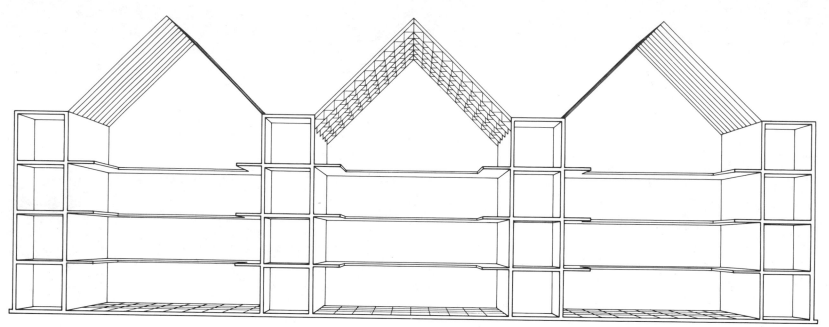

Michael Garber

One-point perspective section

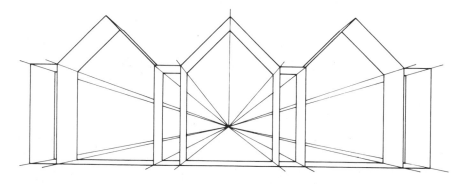

One-point armature

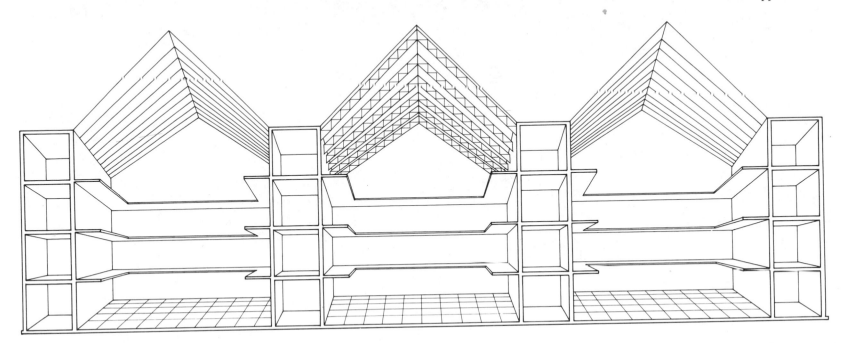

Michael Garber

Vanishing-axis glide section

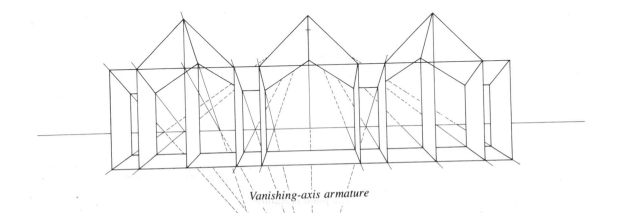

Vanishing-axis armature

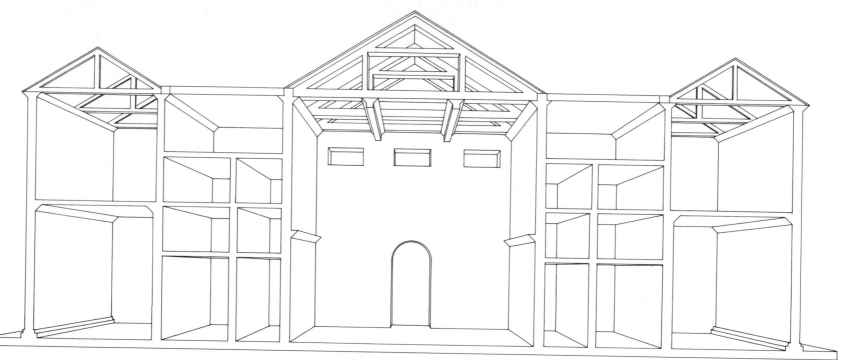

Michael Garber

One-point perspective section, Palladio

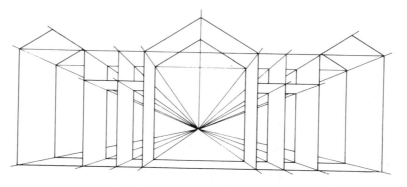

One-point armature

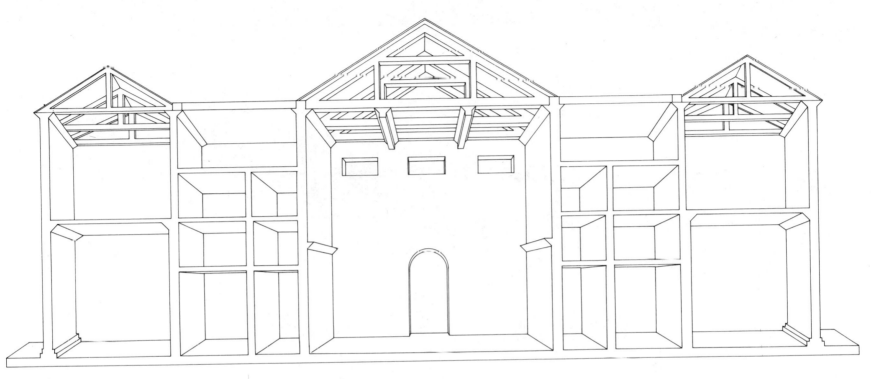

Michael Garber

Double-herringbone glide section

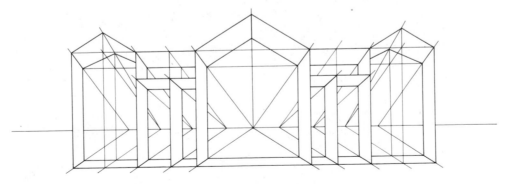

Double-herringbone armature

113

Perspective, Villa Medici, Fiesole

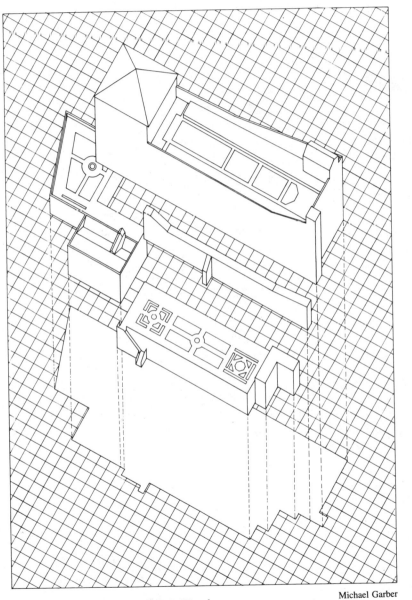

Michael Garber

Exploded paraline, Villa Medici, Fiesole

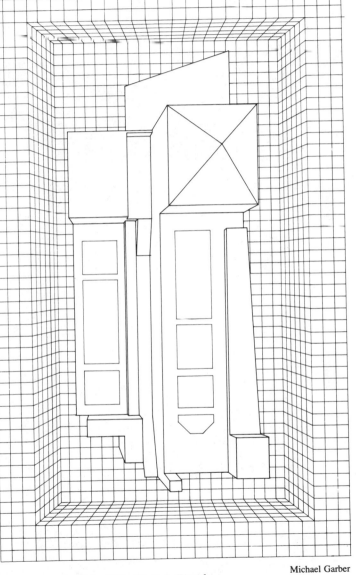

Michael Garber

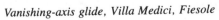

Vanishing-axis glide, Villa Medici, Fiesole

115

Perspective, Villa Lante, Bagnaia

Linda Estkowski

Michael Garber

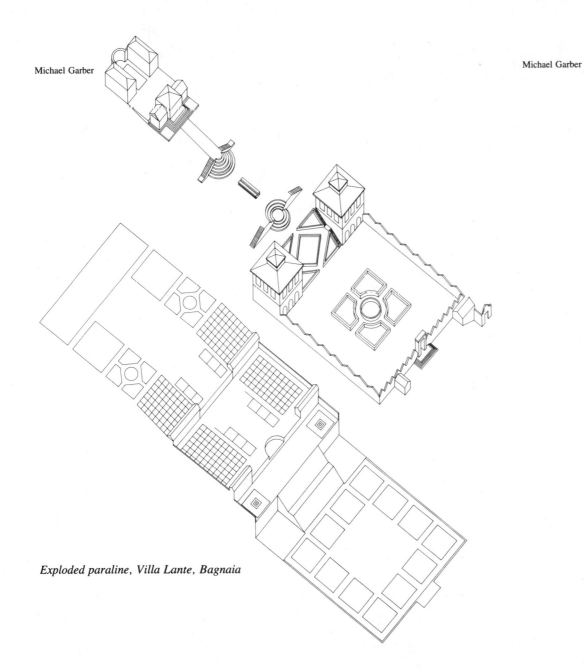

Exploded paraline, Villa Lante, Bagnaia

Michael Garber

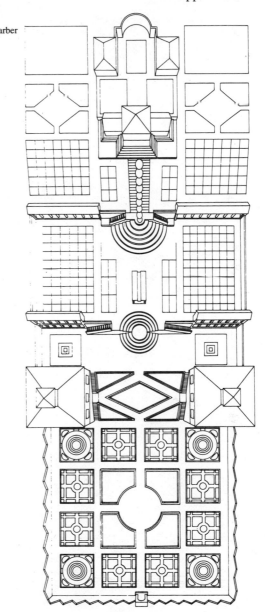

Double-herringbone glide, Villa Lante, Bagnaia

117

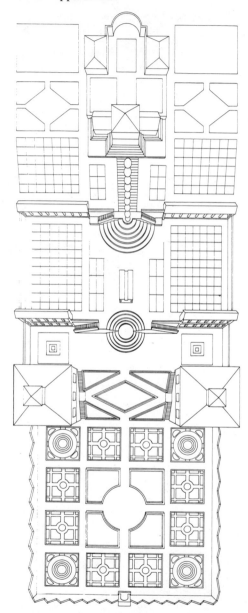

Double-herringbone glide, Villa Lante, Bagnaia

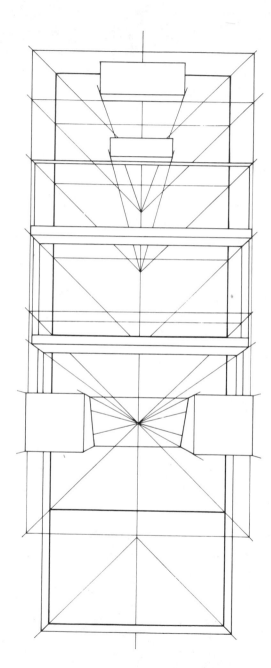

Perspective, Villa di Papa Giulio, Rome

Robert Ruggles

Glide Applications

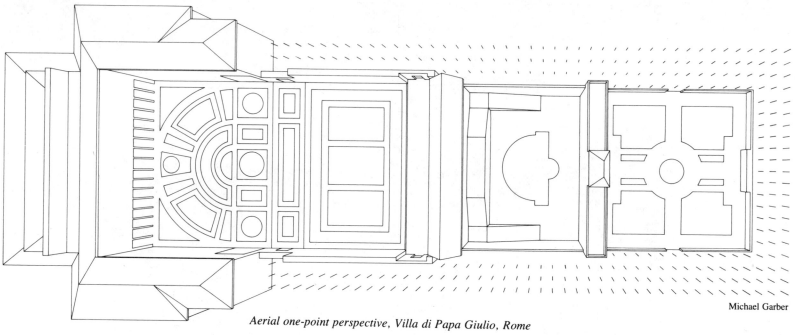

Michael Garber

Aerial one-point perspective, Villa di Papa Giulio, Rome

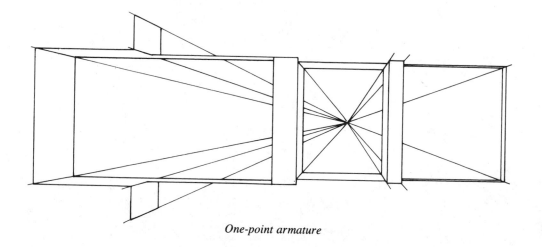

One-point armature

120

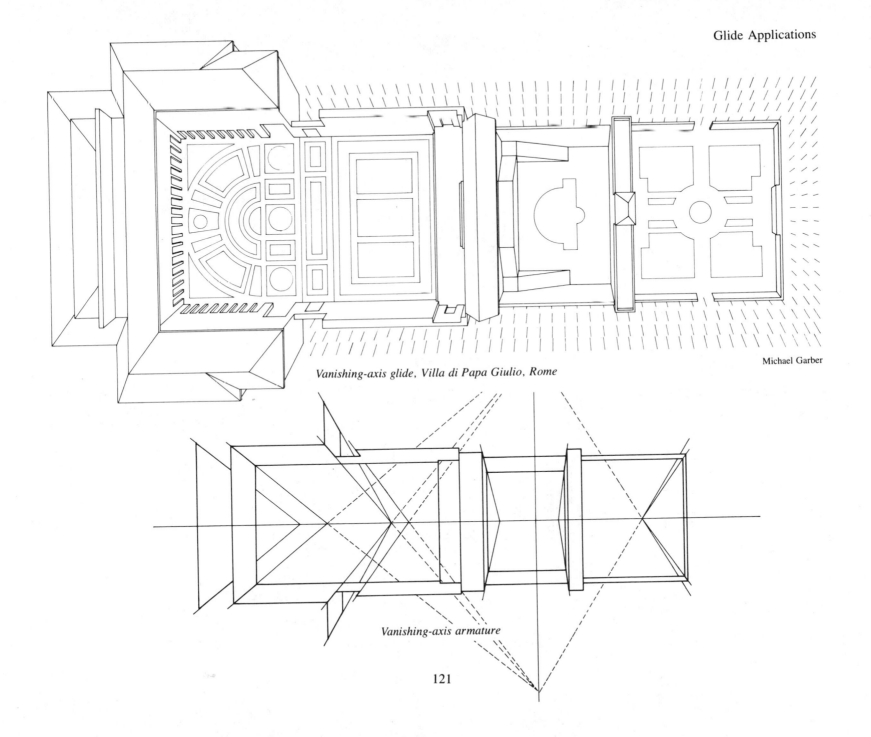

Michael Garber

Vanishing-axis glide, Villa di Papa Giulio, Rome

Vanishing-axis armature

121

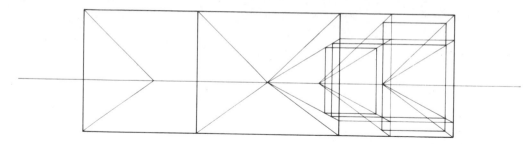

Double-herringbone armature

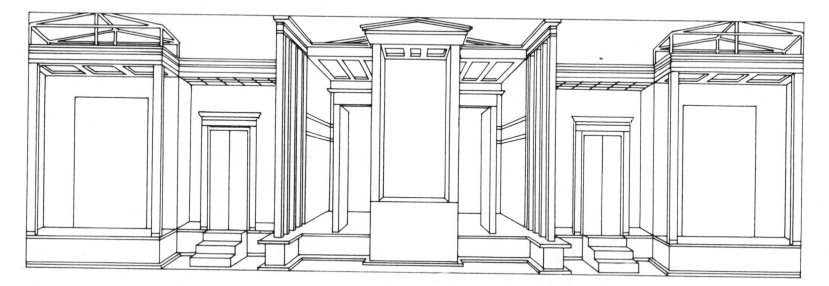

Double-herringbone glide, Pompeiian wall mural

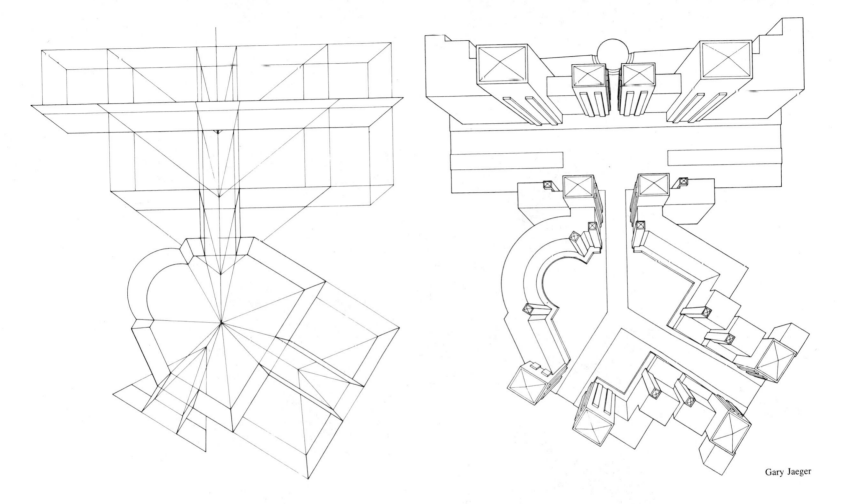

Gary Jaeger

Freeform armature

Freeform glide, scene of plaza

123

Robert Ruggles

Perspective, Villa Medici, Rome

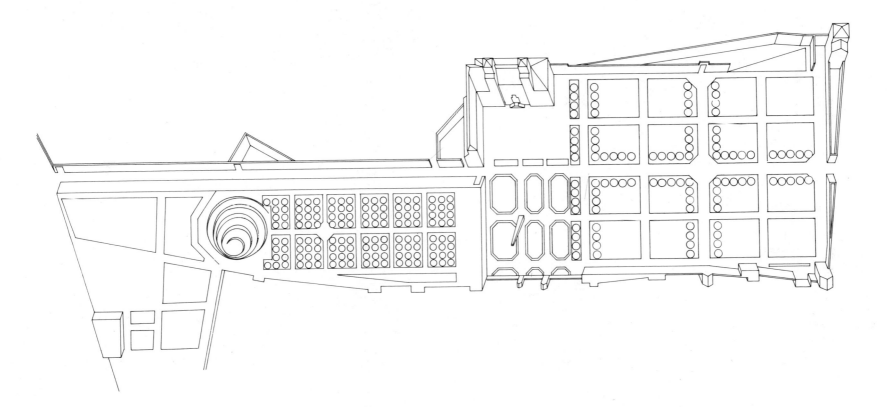

Split axonometric, Villa Medici, Rome

Index